BEHIND THE ILLUSION
DARCY OAKE

An Hachette UK Company
www.hachette.co.uk

First published in Great Britain in 2015 by Cassell Illustrated, a division of
Octopus Publishing Group Ltd
Carmelite House
50 Victoria Embankment
London EC4Y 0DZ
www.octopusbooks.co.uk
www.octopusbooksusa.com

Distributed in Canada by
Canadian Manda Group
664 Annette St.
Toronto, Ontario, Canada M6S 2C8

ISBN 978-1-84403-884-8

A CIP catalogue record for this book is available from the British Library.

Printed and bound in Spain

10 9 8 7 6 5 4 3 2 1

BEHIND THE ILLUSION
DARCY OAKE

UNLOCKING THE 9 TYPES OF MAGIC

CASSELL ILLUSTRATED

CONTENTS

INTRODUCTION

There are a lot of unflattering stereotypes about people who get into magic. When people used to ask me what I did for a living, they'd either mishear me (and think I said 'musician') or they'd ask me to do tricks at their kid's party. Most peope only really started accepting me as a magician when I appeared on television in the UK, in the ITV show *Britain's Got Talent*.

What drew me to magic was simple. I thought it was amazing and I wanted to be able to do it. I was a pretty shy, insecure kid and I wanted people to think I was cool. Social acceptance is why a lot of people get into magic – you fit in, by sticking out. And magic made me feel special. If I went somewhere and felt uncomfortable, or I was in a room where I didn't know anyone, then magic was a comfort. I would think to myself, 'I can do something that nobody else in this room can do.' It was a security blanket.

The practice then was often solitary, so I spent a lot of time in front of the mirror trying to perfect tricks, totally unaware of what was going on in the world. I just wanted to master this amazing thing and it would only occur to me later that I hadn't spoken to anyone in days. In the end, it's not even a conscious choice – you just practise because you know what the final result is going to be. Repeat the action until it's seamless. Then do it again. Everything else just becomes background noise.

I could also see that magic had a weird, time-freezing effect on people. In the moment, it's the most beautiful thing because they forget themselves; they stop thinking about what's going on in their lives and all the things they're worried about. Nobody is thinking about their unpaid credit cards when they're fooled by a graceful effect. Nobody thinks about their unread emails when they see you levitate on a street corner. Magic takes us away from ourselves. And that's a powerful thing.

But it took a long time before magic gave me what I wanted it to (I'm not going to lie, I was kind of hoping I could meet more girls). But after 10–12 years practice, you get there. You also start to work out what kind of magician you want to be. I think it has to take this long because you have to develop as a person before you can actually start saying something with your magic. Between the ages of 17 and 19, I wasn't bold enough; I was just another person

doing tricks. But life happens, doesn't it, and when you mature and have some life experiences you can begin to convey something through your performance. That was always important to me – to have some kind of authenticity – because all the performers I admired had a fully formed identity, they were their own people. That's where I hope I'm at now, and the person on stage doing these crazy things is just a larger version of me, a kid from Winnipeg. I draw inspiration from my life and who I am as a person and, if I get it right, then hopefully you'll believe.

WHY I WROTE THIS BOOK

People always remember the first time they saw a really great magic trick. I think it's important to remember that it can have that effect on people and to recognize what a privilege it is if they tell their grandkids about you. That's why I want to utilize magic in a positive way – it shouldn't just satisfy my pocket or my ego. I see and do magic every day; I eat, sleep, and breathe it, so I don't want to take it for granted. It can be an extremely powerful experience, so you have to be humble.

This is partly why I decided to write something about magic from the audience's point of view. When magic works there's so much at play and it's over so fast; you don't get time to think.

But I love the psychology behind magic tricks, and I love how magic makes you think about the human brain. Above and beyond those seconds of awe or wonder, magic tells us about ourselves. It gives us an insight on how we see the world.

Here's a good example. Imagine you're in front of a close-up card magician and he's asking you to pick a card. How long do you wait before picking? Because honestly, it's not that long. In fact, the length of time it takes everyone to pick – from the shortest amount of time to the longest – is still within a very short timeframe, a second or two at most. You might not have thought before about why that is, or the reason you behave that way. But I have to know why you pick cards quickly, because it might be part of how and why the trick works. Let's face it, we live in a society where there are millions of social constructs that are absolutely second nature to us. So when everyone is looking at you, you don't wait minutes to pick a card, you do it almost straight away, because people are uncomfortable with silence. It's not wrong to be that way, but a magician has to harness these weird facets of human nature.

I also feel like the more we understand the human brain, the better we can feel about ourselves. It's like that comforting feeling you get when a stand-up comedian makes an odd observation about human behaviour; it's a relief to hear that other people do weird things too. When you realize that everyone's kind of strange and that human psychology is full of quirks and strange sidesteps, it's kind of a comfort.

The fact that there's a thirst for people to understand how their brains work is not necessarily a new thing, either. As far back as 1900, a psychologist in Indiana called Norman Triplett came up with a theory of magic that explains all this neatly. He divided magic up into three categories. One, 'Tricks involving scientific principles', two, 'Tricks involving unusual ability or superior information', and three, 'Tricks depending on the use of fixed mental habits in the audience'.

It's that last one I'm interested in. Well over a hundred years ago, we could see that magic involved taking advantage of mental quirks. And it's still relevant now.

All this is important to someone like me because sometimes people see the white teeth, the pretty female assistants, and the pyrotechnics and I wonder if they've forgotten – or simply don't know – how cerebral a form of entertainment magic can be. Magic is entertainment, sure, it's not brain surgery. But what lies behind it are some of the most interesting scientific theories about why humans act as they do. This means that performing magic is sometimes a case of presenting something that's actually science as not-science. And that goes back to an idea that's familiar to (and maybe the curse of) all magicians. To be good at magic, you have to practise indefinitely. But you're practising to hide your skill as opposed to displaying it. It's kind of crazy, because you dedicate your life to learning all this stuff that you can't really talk about it.

What I hope I've come up with is a book that begins to explain more about what happens in a performance of magic – both for me, as a performer, and you, while you're watching it. I'll try not to give away too much about how my illusions are achieved – I'm not a killjoy, I don't want to spoil your fun. But if we look at the history of magic together – both on stage and close up – you'll see that what I do relies on a rich heritage of magic culture that has always exploited and tickled the human brain. They always say there's very little new under the sun, but I would like you to understand why magic will always evolve and should always have the ability to instil a sense of wonder in your heart. No matter how jaded we are.

OUT OF NOWHERE

THE ART OF PRODUCTION

WHAT IS PRODUCTION?

When you think about magicians, the most obvious image is of a man, in tails, pulling a rabbit from a top hat. You've only got to do a Google image search for 'magician' to see this archetype, and it's the classic idea of what someone like me does. I pull rabbits out of hats. Usually really fluffy, white ones. That's why production is one of the best-known and commonly performed kinds of illusion. You've probably seen more production illusions – which are also known as appearance illusions – than any other kind of magic.

Above Ask someone to name a magic trick, and they are most likely to say 'Pulling a rabbit out of a hat'.

Making an animal appear is the most common form of this kind of illusion. At the smaller end, you've got animals like rabbits, mice, or doves. They're often delicate, beautiful creatures, and obviously often they're white, so they're easy to see from the back of the theatre. But some magicians go for the more dangerous large animals, like snakes and tigers. Even elephants used to be a thing back when. Basically, live animals are synonymous with production magic and maybe, on a subconscious level, it's the 'production of life' idea, symbolic of creation.

STATUES THAT SPEAK

Some of the earliest historical accounts of mysterious happenings or miracles involve production illusions. In the temples of ancient Greece, you had urns that would suddenly start pouring wine, statues that could 'talk', and shrine doors that opened by themselves. You can read ancient texts and find out how these illusions were achieved – the machines are amazing, they use pneumatics, simple mechanics, pulleys, and levers, all hidden from view. Some people believe these miracles were just part of the theatre of worship – they were symbolic rituals used to display the gods' powers and designed to make it more exciting to take part in worship. But I'm not sure the audiences were really in on the trick. When you think how little people knew about science, machinery, and automation at the time, I think it's more likely that the ordinary people of ancient Greece thought they were witnessing genuine, spiritual miracles. And that makes the leaders of the temples and the designers of those machines my professional ancestors – they paved the way for people like me to perform my own 'miracles'.

Whatever you believe, we do know that automatons (self-operating machines) have existed since Homer first wrote about tripods that could move by themselves in *The Iliad*. We also know that Hero – a mathematician from ancient Greece – wrote a whole book on devices that could be used in temples to make miracles occur (with or without the knowledge of the congregation). They included a vending machine that would dispense holy water when you inserted a coin and a 'bottomless wine glass' that never got empty. The second one sounds exactly like the sort of thing a magician would want to buy at a convention. Because it's rare for magicians to believe in miracles, they're always looking for the hidden secrets. And sometimes, just sometimes, those hidden secrets and mechanics are just as beautiful as a miracle would be.

Right Hero of Alexandria invented what was essentially the first vending machine: a coin-operated urn that dispensed holy water. To the unsuspecting public, it must have seemed like a miracle.

Opposite Professor Buatier de Kolta on stage with two female assistants, 1902.

BUATIER DE KOLTA

The French magician Buatier de Kolta (1845–1903) invented many tricks, but he is best known today for his pioneering appearance routines involving silk handkerchiefs or billiard balls, which have now become standard tools of the magic trade. In the case of the billiard balls, the performer magically produces a ball in one hand, which then multiplies into three balls, still in the same hand. The style and efficiency of the sleight of hand with which de Kolta performed this trick was incredible – and even though he inspired countless imitations and variations, his original version is still widely thought to be the most impressive.

THE MAGICIAN AS GOD

People have always used magic to make people think they were gods. It's a pure power play, a way for someone to make you believe that they're special and spiritually in touch with something great – a higher power, 'the gods', 'the other side'.

Because some illusions are so effective – and because the kind of people who want to know how tricks work are usually only magicians themselves – many psychic or spiritual illusions still fool people. But they can be dangerous in the wrong hands and I'm thinking of things like psychic surgery here. In psychic surgery, the 'healer' will extract 'toxic' flesh from sick people, claiming to heal them without the aid of a surgeon's scalpel or medicine. To be fair, when performed well, psychic surgery looks kind of amazing, if a bit gruesome. But it's obviously unfair to the genuinely sick who would benefit from real scientific treatment. The great thing is that there has always been a rich vein of people in the magic world who seek to debunk and uncover those who use magic to cheat people out of money or exert power over them. The great magician and sceptic James Randi is perhaps best known for this, offering $1 million to 'anyone who can show, under proper observing conditions, evidence of any paranormal, supernatural, or occult power'.

The distinction and morality of using magic in this way are pretty clear to me. Magic is entertainment, and you have to fool people with good grace. There are performers who treat the audience as if they were the butt of the joke – they go for a cheap laugh any which way they can. But I admire performers who are smarter than that. For one thing, if you're a magician, you're already essentially saying, with every trick, 'I know something you don't know.' And so you have to find a way to perform magic in such a way that the audience enjoys the illusion – and can acknowledge that you have information they don't – and the audience still likes you. You have to keep the secrets of magic with a kind of grace and modesty, and to fool the audience without hurting or embarrassing

'Many psychic or spiritual illusions still fool people... but they can be dangerous in the wrong hands'

Left James Randi, the great magician and sceptic.

them. This is quite a fine line and it goes back to that essential idea that knowledge is power. So you can wield it as a force for good or you can use magic to make yourself look great. What I'm trying to do is to wield it for the enjoyment of everyone in the theatre.

FREE MONEY
& BUCKETS OF FISH

For close-up production illusions, where the audience is nearby, magicians often like to produce money. Maybe you read *Aladdin* as a kid, maybe you didn't – but you can definitely identify with wanting to be able to make stuff appear out of nowhere. You probably even had a cheesy uncle who did a simple version of a production illusion on you, finding a coin magically from behind your ear. But there's an obvious reason why these tricks are still so popular, that relates to who we are as human beings. The fact is, most people wish they could have more money. Rightly or wrongly, we all believe money can solve our problems. So to be able to make $100 bills appear out of thin air is something that really pushes people's buttons. It's total wish fulfillment – we all want to believe it might be possible, even if just for a second.

One of my favourite close-up production illusions was performed by Dynamo with his bucket of fish. It was for one of his specials, *Dynamo: Magician Impossible*, and he filmed it in South Africa. For this

'Rightly or wrongly, we all believe money can solve our problems. So to be able to make $100 bills appear out of thin air is something that really pushes people's buttons'

illusion, he's travelled to a shanty town in Cape Town, and he's got a large crowd around him. He also has a red bucket in his hands, which he shows to the crowd. They can see that it's empty; they can see right to the bottom of that bucket. But suddenly Dynamo turns it upside down and just one fish, about as big as your hand, falls out onto the dusty ground. Then he takes the bucket again, turns it upside down and suddenly ten, twenty, thirty, forty – maybe fifty – fish come out. The way they come out is important, I think, because it's quite slow, as if it's taking time for Dynamo to magically summon these fish before they flop out of the bucket. What I also love is watching the crowd, because they do that laughing and turning away thing ('I can't look! It's too crazy!') and the fish just keep coming and coming. Because there are so many, your brain can't work out how they could even fit in the bucket in the first place, it doesn't add up. That's why the crowd goes wild and it doesn't even matter that they're speaking in Afrikaans or Xhosa – you know they're saying exactly the same things that you or I would. 'What? What?!! How is he doing that?'

Opposite Aladdin conjuring the genie out of his lamp.

THE DOVES

When I performed my Doves illusion on *Britain's Got Talent*, I was really nervous. I'd been working onstage for years, but this was different because I knew that if it went well, things could really change; it would make a huge difference to my life if the judges and the audience liked what I did. It's also one of my favourite routines to perform – the elegance of it, the surprise – and the fact that's it's a classic illusion that a lot of stage magicians have performed before. It's got pedigree; it's the kind of classic magic you really want to do justice to.

Production illusions with doves have been performed by many different magicians over the years. One of the classic performers was Channing Pollock, an American magician and actor who was once billed as 'the most beautiful man in the world'. He was incredibly dapper, suave, and charming and even performed at Grace Kelly's wedding to Prince Rainier. He would produce the doves effortlessly and imperceptibly from red silk handkerchiefs, ending his routine by throwing a dove into the air, down from which tumbled a white kerchief, the dove having vanished. When magicians talk about the Doves illusion, it's often Channing Pollock they picture. But I'm not really like him – I couldn't do that whole top hat and tails thing.

The spin you put on a classic illusion is down to a magician's personal taste. But, as I say, I like to look like myself on stage, so I wear normal clothes – hoodies, leather jacket, jeans, sneakers. My version of the Doves involves a lot of fire, small birdcages

Opposite I prefer to wear my usual clothes when performing, rather than a more old-school look.

that appear out of nowhere and a much bigger production illusion to end the act. I start with a small piece of flash paper which creates a small fire in my hand, but in seconds – and out of the fire – I produce the first bird. I bring my hands together to cradle the dove, but when I pull my hands apart there are two birds, both of which I put into the cage next to me. I produce a white handkerchief that turns into the third dove, by which time there's a large white feather dangling from my mouth. I turn that feather into the fourth dove, which then lays an egg into my hands. I crack that egg to produce a smaller, baby bird, which likes sitting on my shoulder (it's actually a parakeet rather than a baby dove. These birds are very delicate looking but they're quite friendly). I produce some more fire, out of which I conjure a small cage for the baby bird. But in seconds, I've pulled my hands apart to reveal not one, but two, cages, each with a small bird in it. These are given to an assistant. Then it's the big finale, where I cover the large cage with a black cloth. When I take the cloth away, the birds have been replaced by a female assistant in a white dress. The doves have gone.

I can bet that this is not how you remembered that act happening. We'll get to why that's important later on.

WHERE DO THEY COME FROM?

Another classic production illusion would be making a person appear. Your first thought – conscious or not – is obviously, 'Where did they come from?' But a lot of things are happening in your brain at once, and a good magician won't give you too much time to think about this. You certainly won't have time to start discussing what happened with your neighbour. You could also be experiencing a moment of shock or surprise, which means there's adrenaline coursing through your blood, and your heart is beating faster. A fraction of a second later, your eyes start darting all over the stage to see if you can locate the hiding place. There's also music, lights, and smoke – all of which are designed to distract you further.

Your mind is looking for a way out; the human mind likes patterns, because they're easier to file in your brain. But if there is no pattern, you become confused. It's like having a jigsaw puzzle with too many pieces missing. And when this happens, and when you don't get quite understand, 'cognitive dissonance' occurs. Your mind, essentially, gives in. You can't fathom how it's done, so your mind gives you the explanation most desired by magicians. It shuts off and says, 'It's magic!' Here's why.

Above Cognitive dissonance occurs when too many pieces of the (metaphorical) jigsaw are missing.

COGNITIVE DISSONANCE

In the plainest terms, 'cognitive dissonance' is what happens when two conflicting pieces of information or ideas have to coexist in your brain. Let's take an obvious example, which would be people who smoke. People who smoke don't actively want to die. It's also way too simplistic to just say, 'They're stupid'. But they do continue to smoke despite the overwhelming proof that smoking could lead to an early death or terrible form of cancer. Somehow or other, all that damning evidence has entered the smoker's brain. They're even reminded of it every time they look at the cigarette packet. But it hasn't stopped them enjoying smoking. Why?

Early experiments by a social psychologist called Leon Festinger resulted in much of our knowledge of cognitive dissonance. His studies showed that in order for two contradictory ideas to coexist for the smoker ('Smoking is bad'/'I enjoy smoking'), it was natural for smokers not only to distance themselves from information they did not like (health warnings), but to *seek out* information that helped them to reduce this 'dissonance' or 'discomfort' ('I could

Above Despite cigarette packets carrying health warnings, smokers are not deterred – in fact their brains seek out information to distance themselves from the scientific facts.

just as easily get run over by bus tomorrow'/'My granddad smoked every day and lived until he was 80').

In layman's terms, the obvious reason for cognitive dissonance is that life isn't black and white, much as our brains would like it to be. But in the modern world, you come across facts that you can't reconcile and behaviours that can't be explained much less frequently than you might have in the past. You're also much less likely to explain mysterious things by saying 'It's magic' or 'They've got spooky powers' or (as we mention in the Levitation chapter, see pages 54–75) 'They're weird, they're from China'. We're better educated now, we know more about people from around the world, and the minute we want to know about something, we can Google it from our phones or look it up on Wikipedia. In fact, we've come to rely on science and technology to provide our modern sense of wonder, with advances in medicine and space more likely to provide a 'wow moment' than a man with a magic wand.

> 'Life isn't black and white, much as our brains would like it to be. But in the modern world, you come across facts that you can't reconcile and behaviours that can't be explained'

But magic is one area of life where you are forced to encounter things that don't make sense. When you see a feather turn into a dove or one dove turn into two, your brain can't keep up, and you suffer from cognitive dissonance. Your brain can't help it; it needs to let these two ideas ('He has fire in his hand'/'He has a dove in his hand') exist in your brain together at exactly the same time. And this confusion is great for me as a performer, because your brain will supply you with information that helps you sort out this confusion, even if that information is false; you made it up.

YOUR BRAIN ON DOVES

Another reason why people are so fascinated by the Doves illusion is because birds don't feel like controllable animals. They might even make you think of Tippi Hedren being pecked and attacked in Hitchcock's *The Birds* – there's something slightly manic, despite the beauty of birds, by which humans are fascinated. From the magician's point of view, when you're using any live animal that clearly has a mind of its own, this gives the audience some immediate proof that a lot of time and work went into the illusion. Especially if it comes off without a hitch. This is part of its appeal and can make a production illusion more impressive.

If you're fooled by the birds, then it's also down to speed. I'm working faster than you can process the images in front of you. On an irrational level, your mind is fooled because you don't know where the birds are coming from. But if you sat down and thought about it rationally, I feel like everyone knows, really, there's only one place. So another thing I need to do with my performance is to help make sure you don't see them coming from that place. Or make that place seem impossible. I'll do that by using speed and distraction, and by performing the trick in such a way that you look in the wrong place.

But the birds are special because there are so many of them. It's about scale. This means more pressure for me because there are more opportunities for you to see how it's done. Then if I screw it up, you'll not only find out how it works, but you'll also have my mistakes burned into your retina. On the flipside, if I get it right, it's possible that you'll remember there being more birds than there actually were. This misremembering is key to many forms of magic, but I'll begin to explain it here in the context of the birds.

Opposite Birds have a manic energy that fascinates us, and that Alfred Hitchcock tapped into with his 1963 thriller, *The Birds*.

MEMORY & PRODUCTION ILLUSIONS

Your memory obviously affects how you remember a trick, but it's also worth thinking about how this can benefit me. Say you come to see me on tour. Before you arrive, you'll have some idea about what kind of magician I am and the kinds of things that I do on stage. Maybe you've seen some of the illusions before, and so maybe you've had a chance to work out how you think I do them. A lot of people simply don't want to know my methods because they feel it spoils the fun. I get that. But any thinking you've done at all, whether conscious or not, will inform what you look at onstage.

So you get dressed up, you come to the theatre, it's a collective experience. Don't forget that, with that many people in one room, there's also a kind of herd mentality – everyone gasps at the same time, everyone laughs in the same places (hopefully!) – and being part of that experience makes you feel safe on some level; you're part of something bigger than you. Maybe you'll talk about the illusions in the interval over drinks – you think I did it this way, your friend or your husband thinks there must another way, maybe there's a trap door, there are twins. Usually there's one or two people in the audience who are absolutely positive they know exactly how it's all done (they're obviously the most fun to fool). So you go back for the second half, determined to watch harder, closer, more. But some of the theories you've worked out don't quite stand up to scrutiny. You're still looking in the wrong places, and you can't look quickly enough.

The next stage of the process might occur when you're driving home. Your natural instinct – your brain's desire – is to understand and put all the events you just saw into a narrative. This narrative has to a) make sense, and b) sound exciting. It needs to be logical because you need to be able to tell other people at work, on Facebook etc., what you saw without confusing them. And it needs to sound exciting because nobody likes to tell boring stories – nobody wants to be that guy, telling the weird story that doesn't make sense. We all want to be good at telling jokes and to have the best anecdotes.

FALSE MEMORIES

In his brilliant book *The Art of Thinking Clearly*, Rolf Dobelli writes about all the different ways in which our brains are affected by 'cognitive biases'. These cognitive biases are established patterns we can find hard to avoid; they're errors of perception or simple traps of thinking that a lot of us fall into. It's an incredible read but particularly interesting from a magic point of view because Dobelli talks about how fallible our memory is. His writing about how we naturally try to remove discrepancies or glitches from our memory – especially if they don't fit with how we think about ourselves – feeds into a lot of magic.

Right Doug Henning, a fellow Canadian magician, is one of my heroes.

Dobelli says that, in one 1973 experiment, 3,000 people were asked to give their opinion on different controversial subjects, including whether they thought drugs should be legalized. In 1983, he interviewed the same people again, asking them a) to state their current position on the same issues and b) to try to recall what they'd answered ten years ago. What happened was that the majority of people remembered their original answers completely wrong. Because they couldn't imagine thinking differently about these topics, they told researchers that their original opinions were the same as those expressed ten years later. Essentially, we fit our memories around *who we like to think we are*.

How does this fit in with magic? Well, that goes back to the stories you tell other people, the day after my show. And that means we're dealing with another powerful force: your ego. Everyone wants to be liked, everyone wants to be heard, so most people will always lean on the side of *telling the best story*, rather than *telling the real story*. Think about it. If you think of yourself as an entertaining, interesting person (and it's only natural that you would want to), you'll want your account of my show to be more interesting and entertaining than anybody else's. This makes you not only more susceptible to exaggerating ('There were 20 doves!' 'The wall was 2 feet thick!'); it also means you're likely to iron out any of those discrepancies or elements of my show that don't fit in with what you think you saw. And that can be great for publicity!

Here's a great example. Doug Henning – one of my heroes, a brilliant magician from Winnipeg – was performing a show called *Merlin* in New York. After an early show, a newspaper review appeared giving a lot of detail about the illusions Henning performed in the show. The newspaper critic wrote that his favourite trick had been when Henning took a stick and threw it to the ground, where it immediately turned into a boa constrictor and slithered away. Except that's not what happened at all. It's what the reporter – who was right there, presumably with a notebook – remembered seeing. Henning had done something completely different. He had vanished the cane (one illusion), and then produced the snake (an entirely separate one). It may not even have

been a boa constrictor. Our memories lie to us, even if we're being paid to write about what we see.

Magicians aren't immune from making mistakes around memory. When they're learning, a lot of people get confused because they think their magic needs to fool the eye or the mind. But it doesn't. Magic needs to fool the memory. What you believe is happening is what you remember – not reality, not facts. This is why magic doesn't have to just be visual and why it's not just about the illusion per se. When I go through the brick wall (see page 153), you don't actually see me go through it. And that doesn't matter, because a lot of tricks are structured to make sure you forget what really happened.

HOW I MESS WITH MEMORY

The other aspect to all this is that because of what I know about memory, I can influence you more. Magic comprises three things:

1. What really happened
2. What the magician wants you to think is happening
3. What you tell other people

Point 2 here is really important, because I have more leeway than you think. I can influence what you think is happening in many ways. A simple example of this would be when a magician does something while verbally miscalling it. So I might say, 'Here, I want you to just think of a card' and I'll put some cards in front of you, so you can choose one. But I'm saying the word 'think', and I might deliberately use the word 'think' several times throughout the trick; think, think, think, think. 'Now think about the card'. The trick can have many stages and go on for several minutes, and eventually I'll be able to read your mind and tell you what card you thought of.

Later, when you remember the trick or tell your friends about it, you'll say 'He told me to think of a card and then he told me the card I was thinking of!' For reasons of memory, cognitive dissonance, and sheer ego, you may forget to say that I got you to pick your card. Out of a deck of cards that I gave you. My cards,

which I spread out. And that's crucial because it's not impossible for me to get you to pick the card I want you to pick (in magic, this is called a 'force'), a skilled card magician can do that quite easily. In short, mental manipulation is key to a lot of tricks. But because a lot of magic happens in the memory, a lot of the best tricks never even happened.

Above Skilled card magicians can 'force' you to choose the card they want you to pick.

HOW DID THAT GET THERE?

THE ILLUSION OF TRANSPOSITION

WHAT IS TRANSPOSITION?

A transposition is basically a vanish illusion (see pages 98–119) followed swiftly by a production illusion – the magic being that you can make objects or people swap places. The key reason why they're so impressive is to do with speed, and how improbable it is for the magician to disappear behind a red silk cloth onstage, only to reappear at the back of the theatre a moment later. You should be thinking 'What the…?'

What's most important in transposition – whether it's close up (you might make an object leap from one hand to the other) or on stage (where you and a tiger swap places, for example) – is for the audience to know that it's the same person or object before and after the trick. It's so easy to think 'Oh, they used twins', or 'Oh, they've got two of that object' and that's how a sceptic would view this kind of illusion. That's what I most need to disprove throughout my performance so that, instead of looking for twins, you begin to think I'm capable of teleportation. Beam me up, Scotty…

FAMOUS SWITCHES

Transposition illusions take many forms and vary widely in scale. Paul Daniels famously did one in 1985 for his TV show and, though it's largely an escape act, it ends in a brilliant transposition. Paul – chained, shackled, and tied up in a sack – is put into a wooden crate which is lowered by a huge crane into the middle of a racing track. Jackie Stewart (a famous driver of the time) then steps into his car to begin a lap of the course, driving at 120mph towards the wooden crate. When he hits it, the crate explodes in wooden splinters, planks flying everywhere. But the magician has vanished. Then, when the racing driver gets out of the car and takes off his

Opposite In the film *The Prestige*, the magician Alfred Borden (Christian Bale) performs tricks with the help of his twin brother – whose existence is kept secret.

illusion

helmet, it's revealed to be Daniels himself. Jackie Stewart is then shown operating the crane.

David Copperfield is another magician with his own take on transposition. In one, called simply 13, he randomly picks 13 people from the audience (he bounces 13 beach balls around the auditorium, and the people holding the balls when the music stops are picked). His show is performed 'in the round', so the audience surrounds him on all sides. All 13 volunteers are asked onstage to sit on chairs inside a huge, steel-framework cube, and each is given a torch to move so that, when the curtain goes down over the cube, we can still see they're inside. A sheet is brought down over the 13 people and, yes, we see their torch beams waving from behind the sheet. But within seconds, the sheet is pulled back to reveal 13 empty seats. The audience members are now right at the back of the auditorium, happily waving their torches.

Right David Copperfield performs a number of different transposition illusions, one of which, 13, involves members of the audience.

'There are no gimmicks, it's just down to long hours of practice'

CLOSE-UP TELEPORTATION

When you're able to transport an object instantly from one hand to the other without your audience seeing it, you'll find they often lean in. 'Do it again,' they'll say. 'Show me,' they'll ask. People put their faces as close to your hands as is socially acceptable because they're dying to know how you do it.

The classic close-up transposition is called Three Fly. It's a coin trick, usually performed with shiny silver dollars (chosen because, yes, they're shiny, but also because they're pleasingly large, so therefore harder to hide). You start with three coins fanned out in the fingertips of one hand and, one by one, you move them – invisibly – from one hand to the other, without your hands touching. What I love is that it's a beautifully simple illusion. It relies almost entirely on your ability to perform sleight of hand. There are no gimmicks, it's just down to long hours of practice if you want to make it look good. It's another one of those tricks that has existed for a very long time, so those who can still impress with it are extraordinarily skilled.

Above When it comes to sleight of hand, practice really does make perfect.

Overleaf The Sub Trunk illusion is my favourite onstage transposition trick.

'Hopefully the audience is cheering by this point'

SUB TRUNK

My favourite onstage transposition to perform is called Sub Trunk. It begins with the stage bathed in a red light, with a dancing girl draped over a box-shaped object that's been covered with a red sheet. The music is slow and kind of languid, and it has heavy drum beats that punctuate the poses the dancer is making as all of the lights onstage go on and off. In fact, the only light is coming from the floor, with beams shining low across the stage floor. The majority of the theatre is in darkness.

I come on stage in one of those moments of total darkness, pulling the red sheet from the box. This reveals it to be a transparent glass or Perspex cage, about waist high. The dancer goes to grab back the sheet but I wrap her inside it, and we tug it between ourselves before running back to take a corner of the box each. I want to show the audience that the box is real – and that it's not gimmicked – so we spin it full circle, several times, so the audience can see it from all angles. Once it's still again, I pull back the lid, step inside it and sit down. Now you can see how small it is – I can barely sit up inside it, and I can't stretch my legs out.

The lid is then pulled back down, so the dancer can keep it shut using thick, heavy metal chains. The dancer then slowly, calmly, catwalks right to the front of the stage to pick up the sheet and she slowly walks back, dragging it dramatically behind her, all fanned out. I'm completely still (like I say, there's not much room to move in there) and the dancer climbs on top, pulling the sheet up with her arms outstretched, like a huge red cape. She raises it above her head until we can't see her, before it's quickly thrown to one side. But she's not one the one who threw it down: I am. The dancer is now in the locked box and I have to remove the chains to let her out again. Hopefully, the audience is cheering by this point.

For this book, I wanted to try to go some way to explaining what's happening to you when you watch illusions like this. But it's also kind of important that you understand a little of how I feel when I'm up there. To hear people gasp, to hear cheers like

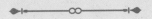

'That simple moment of wonder or awe is a really, really magical moment'

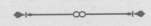

that; there's nothing like it. That simple moment of wonder or awe is – and I don't mean this arrogantly at all – a really, really magical moment, if I pull it off correctly. And when I watch transposition illusions myself, it reminds me of science fiction and fantasy – teleportation devices, the idea that you could be in two places at once, parallel universes, even. I mean, on some level – even if you don't know a whole lot about physics – you wonder if being moved through dimensions or time might one day be how we get to work. Transposition occupies that same imaginative space for me and it's another form of magic that people dream of being able to do. Like when you're at the end of your vacation; you just want to click your fingers and go home. What if you could actually do that?

WE WANT TO BELIEVE: THE MAGICIAN HAS SUPERPOWERS

Read the comments under any magician's YouTube videos, and you'll find several people who claim the magician has some kind of mysterious power. Whether they attribute your abilities to the Illuminati, to voodoo, or the occult, some people really want to believe that there is something sinister going on in magic, that we've all made a deal with the devil. The truth is much more ordinary, and you only need to talk to magicians about how often and for how long they practise their tricks, to get a much less sexy answer. Magic is about practice, so you can hide your method with grace, deftness and sleight of hand. Dolly Parton once said, 'It takes a whole lot of money to look this cheap'. Well I would say, it takes whole a lot of practice to make the impossible look real.

Above Many people claim magicians have mysterious powers, and attribute their abilities to the Illuminati, voodoo, or even the occult.

It has always been this way. Today, we have far more access to information than ever. But way back in history it was more likely that you explained weird phenomena by believing in the spiritual, magical, or mystical. It wasn't possible just to go online and find the answers back then. The fact that we live in a more rational world and the fact that there are fewer bizarre things to believe in (apart from the Illuminati, I guess?), means that magic today is one of the only things you can't explain. Years ago, everything was magic. If you didn't know how something was done, magic was your default explanation. Now we know better and are more cynical, it makes magic even more cherished and special for me. Because it's so rare to see something that you can't explain.

This means that when you perform a transposition, you have to accept that the audience doesn't really believe you can teleport through time and space. But they do need to believe it in the moment, so you have to perform the illusion in such a way that your real secrets, your hidden methods, are not visible. You have to create an atmosphere in which regular, rational sceptical people can still have a moment of awe or wonder, despite the fact that they know you can't move as fast as Superman. Either that, or you give your audience a plausible alternative explanation or theory for what you've just done, and we'll get to why that works that in the Mind Reading chapter (see pages 190–213).

THE PSYCHOLOGY OF TRANSPOSITION

Derren Brown is fantastic at acknowledging that magic doesn't really exist, and at using elements of psychology or say, NLP (neuro-linguistic programming), to explain how he does what he does. What's particularly impressive is that he gives you so much (credible) information and yet still makes his shows hugely enjoyable. This is counterintuitive in a way because, in theory, all those real-world explanations should suck the magic right out of the room. It's a credit to Derren that he can mix theory and illusion so beautifully, and I can't think of a more charming performer. He is so smart.

Opposite Derren Brown performs a brilliant transposition trick involving a man in a gorilla suit.

'[Derren] will also work out personal information about the person... Better still, he's gonna do it blindfold.'

Derren also does one of my favourite transpositions on stage, and what's so charming about it is that it's kind of throwaway, an Easter Egg. It happens just before the interval of his show, *Mind Reader: An Evening of Wonders*. But it's prefaced right at the beginning, when Derren tells the audience about the phenomenon of 'change blindness' (when people fail to see what's right in front of them – we'll look at this in the Transformation chapter, see pages 76–97). Derren tells the audience to watch out for a man in a gorilla suit who will appear at some point during the show. The gorilla will try and steal a banana and the audience must shout when they see him. This is great because most people, at that point, are going to want to be the one to spot the gorilla first. It plays a little into our competitive spirit. Derren gets on with the show.

Later, right before the interval – and after a fantastic prediction trick – Derren is telling the audience about a 1930s mind-reading act called The Oracle, that he intends to perform when they come back for the second half. To prepare, the audience needs to think of 'personal and private' questions they would like answered ('Should I take that new job? Should I get married?'). They need to write them down and seal them in envelopes which will be placed in a bowl on stage. He tells them they're not even allowed to tell their partners or friends what their questions are. When they come back after the interval, he will not only be able to deduce what their questions are (without opening the envelopes); he will also work out personal information about the person who wrote each question. Better still, he's gonna do it blindfold.

Derren follows this prep-speech with the conclusion of an earlier trick where an audience member is asked to choose whether he thinks a covered box contains £500 or £5,000. If he's right, he can have the contents of the box. Unsurprisingly, he gets it wrong. But by now the audience is pretty hopped up. They're feeling all the feels – what personal or emotional questions should they ask? How can they get to the bar first? And they're clapping and laughing because the man has failed to win the money (just as Derren predicted). In the midst of all this, Derren starts fiddling with props onstage. He moves a large easel from stage left to stage right, and is obscured behind it. Meanwhile – suddenly – the gorilla appears (stage left) to grab the banana. 'Oh no! I'm so sorry,' says Derren. 'I shouldn't have let that happen.' But then the gorilla takes off his mask. It's Derren.

BEGINNINGS, MIDDLES & ENDS

Sometimes the mark of a great trick is when you hear someone recount it to you. And if you've ever met anyone that saw Derren's gorilla switch, you'll know what they said. 'He was on stage the whole time!' or, 'But, he couldn't have…' This is the mark of a fantastic transposition. It also goes back to that idea of narrative, and how our brains like to fit what we see into a simple story, a story that can be easily retold. This means that when our brains encounter something that does not conform to the narrative – or that doesn't make sense – we tend to misremember or mis-see it. In Derren's case, he's outlined the narrative at the beginning of the show. The story is: you need to look for the gorilla. What he's not telling you to do, of course, is to keep your eyes on him.

Left Anyone who has seen Derren Brown perform his gorilla switch will say, 'He was onstage the whole time!'

THE ATTENTIONAL BLINK

Psychologists are fascinated by misdirection and how magicians use the way our brains work to fool us. They're particularly interested in how different forms of misdirection and magic can harness our powers of perception; how we see, hear, and touch things and how fast our brains can use this information – process it – to tell us what we're seeing. They're interested because sometimes there's a disconnect between what we perceive and what actually happened. This can often happen when our brains are trying to process lots of information at speed, and the speed makes us miss important information, even though it's right in front of us. One example of this phenomenon is called the 'attentional blink'. It's less complicated than it sounds, and concerns how quickly your brain can process information when you're looking at something fast.

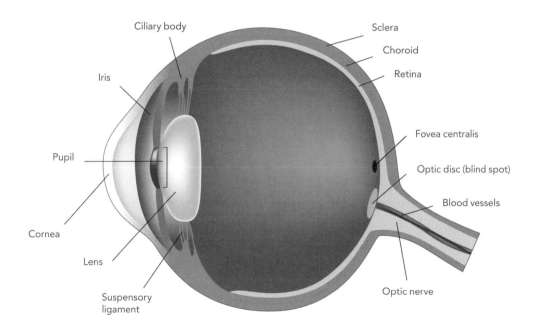

In experiments, people are shown a series of images very quickly (say, a series of letters, one at a time, on a computer). As the letters flash before their eyes, participants are asked to identify two numbers that could appear at any time among the letters. What

Above Humans have a physical blind spot, which magicians rely on, and a perceptual blind spot, which causes the attentional blink.

Opposite Sportsmen use misdirection in the form of 'dummy' passes, sending their opponents in the wrong direction in order to leave themselves unmarked.

scientists wanted to uncover was not just whether people could see numbers in among a stream of letters. They also wanted to know how quickly they could spot them and if it made a difference how soon the second number appeared after the first. When the brain is looking for more than one thing, how long does it need to recover before it can spot the next?

What they discovered is that there are blind spots in our perception. When the second number was shown soon after the first number, people were much less likely to spot it or remember it. What they experienced was a kind of lag or 'blink' in their ability to process the second number. It was almost as if the energy needed to spot the first meant that their brain was in a kind of recovery period just after. And, in that recovery period, people missed the second number. Basically, our brains aren't quick enough.

What's crazy is that this 'blink' – this lapse in our ability to see important information – is also affected by emotion or stress. Simply, stress can make us perceive and remember things better, and emotion makes it harder. This was demonstrated in a 2010 study where volunteers were asked to participate in a test similar to the one above. Each person was shown a sequence of 15 words on a computer screen – 13 were written in white, 2 in red. All the volunteers had to do was to identify the two red words. The difference was that the researchers wanted to see if emotion or stress could affect this 'blink'.

In the 'stress' version, volunteers had to plunge their hand into very cold water (making their bodies produce cortisol, the stress hormone) before taking the test. In the 'emotional' version, the red words were replaced with 'aversive words', words that provoke an emotional response (they used words like 'bitch' or 'bastard'). By measuring how well the participants were able to pass the test when stressed or emotional, they came up with two basic findings: 1. Stressed volunteers were more likely to spot the second red word than those who were not; 2. Volunteers who were in an emotional state after reading the first red emotional word would be even less likely to spot the second.

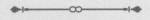

'There are blind spots in our perception. Basically, our brains aren't quick enough'

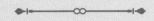

Opposite Harry Houdini and his wife, Bessie, helped make the Metamorphosis illusion famous.

METAMORPHOSIS

Metamorphosis is a stage illusion originally created by John Nevil Maskelyne, but today we mostly know of it thanks to Harry Houdini, who first performed it with his wife Bessie in 1894. More recently, The Pendragons became famous for the incredible speed with which they performed this illusion. Houdini was locked in a large trunk, tied up in a sack with his hands secured behind his back. His wife drew a curtain, covering the trunk and herself, and clapped three times. The curtain was then drawn back again by Houdini himself, and Bessie was the one who was now tied up in the trunk.

USING YOUR BRAIN BLINK

Illusion tricks aren't just about science though – there wouldn't be much point in an audience being there if they were – so enough science, let's relate all this to magic. Think about a transposition illusion – or a transformation, for that matter. In a performance of Sub Trunk, speed is of the essence – there isn't a trick without it. So if I am able to hide my secret method quickly enough or build it into a sequence of movements that rapidly follow one another, and make sure that my performance has some form of emotional element (by, say, talking about my life), then it's very unlikely you'll be able to detect my secrets. If I want you to remember something (especially if it leads you away from my secrets), I can use simple, stress-inducing effects like pyrotechnics, fire, flashing lights, or sudden bursts of sound.

Then, when I want you to forget (or miss) what I'm doing, I'll use emotion. Personal stories, sad or happy elements, dancing, music – whatever it takes to make you feel. And all of those elements take time to perform. Which is why I don't walk right on stage, get in a box, and switch places with a dancer. It's why all magic is about context and presentation. You'll see everything I do in the literal sense, because it's right there in front of you. But it won't register in your consciousness. As as far as you're concerned, it doesn't exist.

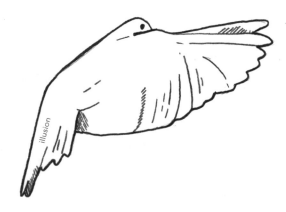

illusion

WALKING
ON AIR

LEVITATION AND THE SCIENCE BEHIND IT

THE MAGIC OF FLIGHT

Illusion based on levitation or suspension holds the same allure
for both the magician and the audience. Like disappearance (see
pages 98–179) and mind reading (see pages 190–213), being able
to levitate is a superpower that zeroes into one of humanity's most
common desires – being able to fly. We've all dreamed about it –
those perfect moments when you can transcend the limitations of
your body and leap over obstacles, soaring high above everyone.
Even now, students of lucid dreaming (that is to say, dreaming while
you're aware that you're dreaming) practise for years to be able to
access this feeling, with some claiming to truly leave their bodies.

'We've all dreamed about it – those
perfect moments when you can transcend
the limitations of your body'

THE INDIAN ROPE TRICK

In magic, levitation and suspension routines have a rich history, with
accounts of the Indian Rope Trick dating as far back as the ninth
century. In early descriptions, the conjuror or mystic – accompanied
by a small boy – has a large basket and a huge ball of thick rope.
The rope is sent so far into the sky that it defies physics. You can't
see the end of it and it stays upright and vertical. The boy is sent
climbing up the rope until he's also eventually lost from view.
In some stories, he's climbing to fetch delicious peaches from
heaven, because it's winter and there is no fruit. In others, he simply
disobeys the magician, refusing to come down when called. So
the magician is forced to follow the boy up the rope, eventually
disappearing into the clouds himself.

Opposite Harry Kellar, an American
illusionist of the late-19th and early-20th
centuries, performing a levitation trick.

What happens next is both magical and macabre. In the 'peaches' version of the story, the boy is discovered in heaven and chased out by guards who slice off his limbs, sending arms and legs flying down from the skies. In the 'naughty boy' version, it's the magician who cuts off the boy's limbs, angry that he was disobeyed. Finally, the magician returns down the rope, putting the disembodied legs, arms, and head into the basket. He then puts the lid on the basket and pauses, before the boy emerges out of the basket, completely unharmed.

Obviously, this sounds like the ultimate illusion. Performed outdoors – with no stage to conceal levers and pulleys – audiences would go ballistic. And if I learned to do it, I'd be richer than Simon Cowell. The trouble is, it never happened. Like so many illusions, the hype surrounding those early versions of the Indian Rope Trick is what makes it so popular – it's why I'm still writing about it today. But that hype comes from the most unreliable witnesses on earth – human beings. And so we now believe that those early accounts are amalgamations of people's memories of different illusions. But because people nearly always remember tricks wrong, we have this crazy version of the Indian Rope Trick, which was repeated, over and over, like an urban legend. For illusionists like me, that's no bad thing. Misremembered tricks are the key to a lot of magic and the fact that you'll remember my illusions slightly differently – the sequence of events, how high I floated, how many doves I produced – can make what you tell people you saw at my show quite different to what actually happened. If I can build elements into my show that help make you remember things wrong, so much the better.

illusion

Above The Indian Rope Trick is one of the oldest known illusions.

Opposite Howard Thurston, one of the most famous magicians of his time, performed his own take on the rope trick.

THURSTON
THE FAMOUS
MAGICIAN
EAST INDIAN
ROPE-TRICK
World's Most
Famous Illusion
First Time-out-of
India
REAL INDIAN CONJURORS
THE WORLD'S FAMOUS MYSTERY

FLOATING MEN & DOLLAR BILLS

Illusion effects performed in close-up can be harder to perform than levitations that happen on stage. There's the obvious problem that you're too close to me; I can't control where you're sitting because there are no theatre seats, and I can't stop people walking down the street and seeing what I'm doing at close quarters. Plus, if I make a dollar bill float between my palms, your natural instinct is going to be to lean in and get closer. You're gonna look – hard – at what I'm doing because it's so incredible; it shouldn't be happening. That disbelief is as useful to me as a performer as your poor memory, and we'll get to that later. But I can tell you that seeing that disbelief in someone's face is just one of the things that make close-up levitations so fun to perform. If I get it right – and you can't see how I'm doing it – I'm gonna blow your mind.

David Blaine is obviously the master at this. His street levitations were on camera, to groups of real people in New York who went absolutely crazy. What's great is that you get to see all the different reactions that illusions like levitation provoke in people – the full spectrum, from ruffled brows to full-on hysterics. Some people even turn or run away because they can't compute what they're seeing. Most of them start laughing. One girl says, 'My heart is pounding.' Another is doubled over, she can't speak. One – which is so perfect – comes up with a classic interpretation for things-we-can't-explain – Blaine is channelling the spirits. She says, 'I've read up on this stuff…I guess he's very gifted. Spiritually, he's very gifted.' My favourite, though, involves three girls in New York he levitates for. In cities like New York, people are famously hard to impress. It's a tough place, where people mind their own business; they've seen it all before. But one girl just keeps saying, 'He floated. He floated. Did you see him float? He floated. It wasn't no TV scam. He floated.' That's as real a reaction as you're going to get, and it's what people like me live for.

THE FLOATING VANISH

On stage, it's always going to be harder to make a levitation truly impressive. There are lots of reasons why this is so, but let's start with the obvious: you're living in the modern world and though you'd like to believe it's possible, you know I can't really float. You've also seen people 'fly' before, using wires on stage – cheesy performances of *Peter Pan* with thick steel ropes that can easily be seen, that kind of thing. Because you think you know how it works, you're harder to impress. But that just means I have to work harder, and your scepticism is something I'll just have to take into account when I plan my performance.

My levitation is inspired by Servais Le Roy's classic act, which was first performed in London in 1914. The person being levitated is hypnotized by the magician in some way, so that they are in a kind of trance. The hypnotized person will then faint or lie back, at which point they will be laid on a table, as if in a coma. A sheet is placed over them, and it'll look rather like how we cover up dead people – and if it reminds you of that, that's no accident – before the magician commands the table to rise high into the air, way above his head. The magician himself then floats upwards, or jumps, pulling at the sheet so that it tumbles down. As the silk dramatically falls away, it is revealed that the hypnotized person has vanished into thin air.

Done well, Le Roy's levitation is a beautiful mixture of the strange and surprising. You don't know what's coming, so the vanish at the end is a startling punchline. That's partly what I love about it – it's two illusions in one: a levitation and a disappearance. But if you perform magic, you have to try to evolve what you're doing constantly, so that it still feels relevant to a modern audience. I wanted to put my own spin on the floating vanish and perform something that felt real. I also wanted to bring my own story into the performance because I like my magic to have a personal edge. Here's how I do it:

On stage, I narrate a true story as two male dancers perform a piece about the characters. The story that is woven into this

Opposite I perform my own interpretation of Servais Le Roy's classic levitation.

'Done well, this illusion is a beautiful mixture of the strange and surprising'

illusion is about two brothers. One is 'the alpha of the two, larger than life, spontaneous and with a magnetic personality'. The other is 'younger, a bit more shy, awkward, a little insecure. Yet, wildly ambitious.' The two brothers are best friends, but they choose to follow dramatically different paths in life – the older brother choosing to live dangerously fast. Tragically, the older brother dies – one of the dancers falls back – leaving the younger brother alone, carrying his body.

'You have to try to evolve constantly so that it still feels relevant to a modern audience'

My assistants put the dancer/brother on the table, where his arms are crossed and he's covered with a silky sheet. The music swells – and as he rises up, horizontal, the assistants remove the table. He's way, way up now, in the upper reaches of the stage, with the sheet billowing under the lights. I move to the back of the stage and levitate vertically, gracefully. Then I float back down, pulling the sheet with me. The man has gone. And the man, of course, is my brother, Bruce.

He died of a drug overdose in 2011. I miss him every day.

Opposite Servais Le Roy and his wife, Talman, performed their levitation act for the first time in 1914, in London.

64

DEFYING YOUR BRAIN

To understand why you're fooled, or – at the very least – entertained by a levitation illusion, you have to understand a few things. First and foremost, there's a fairly obvious technical problem I need to overcome. It's incredibly important that all of the movement is graceful – you have to make it look as if someone is really floating. There's an art form to the mechanics of it, because you need to look weightless: the ideal levitation will make it look like you're moving in zero gravity. I need to trick your brain into going along for the ride.

Right Robert Harbin perfoms levitation with the help of sunbathers on a beach in Eastbourne, UK.

A GIFT FROM THE GODS TO MORTALS ON EARTH TO AMUSE AND MYSTIFY.

CHUNG LING SOO

THE EXOTIC IN HISTORY

There are also powerful historical reasons why levitations are so popular. When Servais Le Roy was performing his ground-breaking act in the early 1900s, the idea of hypnotism was still new and mysterious. It had even been aligned with strange spiritual practices like voluntary burial, self-hypnotism, and human hibernation. It was deemed a puzzling unknown. Crucially, hypnotism was an idea that reached Western audiences from the Orient – and magic has always played with ideas of the exotic. Far-off places like China were unknown to audiences then, and there was a persistent idea that the people of the East were mystical and powerful in strange new ways. From a psychological point of view, the idea that hypnotism was from the East lent it a certain credibility – or at the very least, allowed showmen and magicians to give the audience a plausible

Above In the early 1900s, American magician William Ellsworth Robinson called himself Chung Ling Soo and pretended to be Chinese.

narrative for their illusions; one that the audience was unlikely to question. An American magician, William Ellsworth Robinson, even went so far as to pretend to be Chinese for his act, making up his face, hair, and costume and calling himself Chung Ling Soo. It's unthinkable today. But it does prove one thing – that a magician will use any ideas you're not expertly familiar with, if he or she thinks it will make their act seem real or somehow plausible. Just enough mysticism, just enough unknown, helps your brain feel like you already have an explanation for what you're seeing.

So, for similar reasons, magicians are drawn to science. Though most have a basic understanding of scientific principles, sadly few of us are smart enough to study physics, chemistry, maths, or biology in academic detail. And you can bet your life that all magicians know this, and use it to their advantage. This has been going on for as long as magic has been performed. For example, Robert-Houdin's levitation illusion – the Ethereal Suspension (1847) – used the unknown properties of the anaesthetic ether to explain

illusion

how he could make his own six-year-old son fall into a hypnotic sleep, before being floated horizontally, apparently only supported by his elbow. No one really knew what ether did, so the audience was able to accept 'ether' as a partial explanation for the spooky goings-on.

There's also a levitation illusion that involves a child being suspended in the air by a bunch of huge helium balloons. The idea here is that the magician is giving your brain an explanation for something that shouldn't be happening. Children should not be able to float, but maybe, just maybe, if you give them enough balloons, they will. An illusion needs a motivation. If the child was just leaning back in a chair at some impossible, gravity-defying angle, it would look crazy, an interesting visual. But you would not be able to shut up that part of your brain that asks, 'How is this happening?' or 'Why is it happening?' The second you put a balloon in the kid's hands, your brain plays along a little more, and that little voice will be much more likely to say, 'Oh, it's the balloon holding him up. How magical!' It's not just an odd visual, it's not just a trick. Part of the way you'll allow someone like me to fool you with magic is because there's a relevance and a motivation for what's happening. If there's a reason for why something is happening in magic, you have a show.

Above Performing a widely publicized levitation trick, British magician Dynamo walked on the river Thames in London.

Opposite In the mid-19th century, Robert-Houdin made his six-year-old son levitate in The Ethereal Suspension.

HARNESSING YOUR DESIRES

Another thing to remember when you're watching a levitation illusion is that magicians like me have a certain amount of good will on our side. Earlier, I talked about how common it is for people to dream of having superpowers. Most people would like to be able to do the same, fantastic, things – to fly, to walk through walls, to read minds, or predict the future. These are classic desires that many of us share and that a lot of storytelling taps into. The millions of adults who read Harry Potter books were more than happy to suspend their disbelief if it meant they could enjoy imagining what it would be like to cast spells on themselves or other people. Look at how many superhero movies have been made in the last 20 years, too. They're popular for similar reasons and of course, magicians do things that superheroes do – we fly, we walk through walls, we disappear. This kind of escapism is a healthy part of entertainment, it takes us out of ourselves and lets us forget everyday life, even it's just for a moment. But that willingness to escape – the fact that you want to believe I can do these superhuman things, loosens you up and makes you easier to exploit psychologically.

So the smart magicians will harness these desires and exploit them. They will use the fact that, while you're watching, you're in an open, imaginative, and hopeful state. Subconsciously or consciously, you're thinking about swapping places with me on stage, and being able to do what I do. And that's exactly what I need you to be doing, because if your imagination kicks into gear, it's much more easy for me to misdirect you. You're more easily manipulated. Misdirection is useful in nearly all forms of magic, but when you're performing something as unbelievable and flat out crazy as a levitation, you need there to be as many mental distractions as possible. That way, you quieten down the clinical, rational part of your brain. And that way, it's easier for me to make you look at the wrong things.

Opposite Most of us would love to have superpowers of some sort, especially the ability to fly.

illusion

MISDIRECTION & LEVITATION

The other aspect to misdirection is that there's something quite primal about our desire to mirror each other's actions. There's a reason why you look where I look, or look where I point, or look to where the lights are pointing. Let's imagine we're all still living in caves, wearing our animal skins. We're a tribe, we need to work together if we want to stay alive. So if I see a sabre-toothed tiger, I'm gonna look at it, and you can read the alarm in my face, which prompts you to look where I'm looking. So you'll look too, and then maybe we'll have a chance at outrunning that thing. I think it's in our nature to do this. People follow other people's direction of gaze, presuming there must be something interesting to look at. Maybe it's danger, maybe it's food, maybe it's a sexy girl – but if everybody else is looking at something, you're automatically interested.

A good example of this is when I was at school. People used to play this game – which was wildly immature, granted – but they would go to the mall, throw a hat down on the floor, and then just stare at it. And then we would wait to see how long it would take before other people would come and stand next to us and watch the hat too. Within 15 minutes, you'd have maybe 20 or 30 people standing around, looking at you, looking at a hat. It's entirely possible that this taps into something evolutionary, that our instinct is to use other people as a cue for how we behave ourselves. This herd instinct works exactly the same way if you stand in the middle of the street and look up at the sky. Social conditioning and the remnants of our primal brain can make fools of us all.

When I perform my own levitation, I'm also using storytelling techniques. This is partly because I like my magic to be personal and to reflect who I am. If it doesn't sound too pretentious, I also want my show to mean something; I don't want to be a faceless, cheesy guy on stage showing off. That idea has to inform the whole of my performance, from the music to what I wear and how I speak. The few seconds where I actually levitate are such a small part of my performance, so for me to influence how you remember

Opposite We tend to follow other people's gazes, presuming there must be something interesting to look at.

it and how you're gonna describe it to your friends is what really counts. And you need a narrative, because the human mind runs on stories. Using a story is so common in magic. You're often told ahead of time at the beginning of an illusion what's about to happen – and without going into too much detail, that's partly so that you remember what I said happened, rather than what actually did. It's also a bit like the classic idea of a Bond villain, who explains his dastardly plans to 007 before he offs him with a nuclear laser. Telling you what's going to happen creates expectation in your mind, and your brain will immediately start whirring and projecting ahead, working out how it will happen, and when. And that projecting ahead? It's another way for me to keep your brain busy while I trick you.

The difference with a levitation illusion, however, is that you need to subvert that narrative a little bit. This is because the levitation itself should come as a surprise to the audience. I mean, I need you to gasp when it happens, or I haven't done my job. And as in any form of magic, if you aren't sure what's about to happen next, you can be sure you won't spot it. I need to be one step ahead of you at all times, because then you'll be easier to manipulate and misdirect. Magic is unlike most forms of entertainment in this way – when you sit down in the auditorium, you have no idea what the 'plot' of the evening is going to be. That's good for you, because you get to have a surprising evening. And it's great for me, because I'm miles ahead of you, and I know where we're going.

'I need to be one step ahead of you at all times, because then you'll be easier to misdirect'

COGNITIVE BIAS

The last thing that's key in levitation is a little idea called 'cognitive bias'. What this means is that the human brain tends to look for answers in the place we expect them to be. We often process new experiences based on all the old ones we've had, which means there are a lot of learned behaviours and patterns that are very well entrenched by the time we become adults.

So when you see a levitation illusion, subconsciously your brain is running through all the other times you've come across something remotely similar (something being pulled into the air, even your knowledge of how gravity works). This means that in a close-up levitation, you're looking at that dollar bill floating between my hands and – based on all the billions of images and experiences you've already seen and heard, and that your brain has already processed – you have expectations (or biases) for where the wires must be. You're no fool, you know how things get lifted up in the air – it's from above, right?

Right.

Above The levitation itself should come
as a surprise to the audience.

METAMORPHOSIS

TRANSFORMATION ILLUSIONS

WHAT IS TRANSFORMATION?

The most powerful magic is also often the clearest; when the clarity of the effect is absolute. What I mean is that there can be no simpler, more complete illusion than 'the man turned into a tiger'. When the audience can explain what happened in words of one syllable and in one sentence, you have clarity. Unfortunately, the simplest illusions are often the hardest to pull off, and the fact that they're uncomplicated means that there'll be much more pressure on the magician; no room to hide. Many transformations have this purity and simplicity in common, and what they rely on is deftness and speed.

I guess the most famous transformation would be when Jesus turned the water into wine (there's a good few people who think he was a magician, too). I guess for sheer romanticism you can't beat Cinderella's pumpkin and it's magical transformation into the carriage that takes her to the ball. The enduring power of both these stories should give you some idea as to why transformation magic is still performed, but there's also the fact that it's such a broad, flexible category of magic. Depending on the method, you can turn pretty much anything into anything else.

The Greeks gave us King Midas, whose ability to transform everything he touched into gold meant he killed his daughter. Despite the tragic end, most people are happy to spend a good few seconds imagining how incredible a power like that would be (let's face it, we all have winning-the-lottery fantasies). It means, yet again, that with transformations you have the audience with you, because they want to believe you can do it. It taps into our irredeemable hope that magic is real – and that if we could do it, we'd be so rich we'd never run out of money. Part of the appeal of being a magician is that you get to see that delight in people's faces, that millisecond where they truly believe you can change coal into diamonds.

Opposite Cinderella's pumpkin being turned into a carriage is a magical transformation.

MONEY, MONEY, MONEY

People often believe that if they were just close enough to the magician – if they got to occupy the spot right in front of him – they'd be able to see how it's done. But when you're dealing with David Blaine, you've got no chance. So one of my favourite close-up transformations has to be when he transformed a $1 bill into $100 on a street corner.

He's doing the trick for four young men, and he gets them to promise that if he's able to change the bill to $100, they'll split it four ways between them. Then he folds the bill and puts it into the hand of one of the boys, putting his hands around the boy's clenched-tight fist. Now he's quiet, not saying anything, just pushing hard on the boy's fist from all angles as if he's channelling his magic, doing something spooky. 'Did you feel that?' he asks when he's stopped moving his hands. 'AMEN!' shouts one of the boys. But as soon as he lets them take a look, one of them grabs the note, screams and runs off at high speed, followed by the others. Basically, there's no way they're giving that money back. In fact, what's so great is that you can hear Blaine's crew on the tape, laughing it up. The camera stays on the boys as they vanish into the distance. Their reaction is so spectacular, we don't even get to see if the trick has worked.

Above People think that if they're close to a magician they'll see how a trick is done – with David Blaine, you've got no chance.

Opposite David and Dania are famous for the speed of their transformation acts.

QUICK CHANGE TRICKS

Quick Change tricks involve magicians changing their outfits in front of the audience as good as instantaneously. Two performers famous for the speed of their transformations are David and Dania, who appeared on the first season of *America's Got Talent*. They have ten different transformations in their performance, and use a variety of transitions to switch from one costume to another, including dropping a hoop over the performer's body, walking through a cabinet and being showered with glitter. Their performance is all the more impressive as the costume changes don't seem to allow any time for a mechanism to be used or an action to take place – and the duo never miss a beat.

QUICK CHANGE

On stage, magicians often harness the power of scale, or invoke a bit of danger. This means you're dealing with huge circus animals, like Siegfried & Roy's tigers, which magically turn into people, or vice versa. They're powerful illusions precisely because people find it hard to work out how on earth you could get an animal that wild, or that large, into a theatre – never mind have it disappear and change places with a magician. It's no accident that Siegfried (Fischbacher) & Roy (Horn) chose tigers, either. When you think about how the internet basically runs on cats, and how they have fascinated us going right back to the Egyptians, we can't help but be spellbound by these elegant, beautiful, and wild creatures. Siegfried & Roy, of course, found out to their cost just how dangerous even well-trained animals can be. In 2003, during what tragically became one of their last-ever shows, Roy was bitten on the neck by one of their male tigers and dragged offstage. He survived, but it took him years to learn to speak and walk again.

Right Siegfried & Roy have famously made tigers turn into people, and vice versa.

illusion

At the other end of the spectrum you've got costume transformations. The most famous example would be Sos and Victoria Petrosyan, a husband and wife team who devoted their lives to becoming the slickest and fastest quick-change act in the world. They're four-times Guinness world-record breakers (their last, in 2011, was for 13 costume changes in 1 minute), and their act has taken them around the world. I don't really need to explain what happens, but it's worth thinking about why we're mesmerized by these kinds of performances. I think it's got a lot to do with fairly simple ideas like awe, or wonder, and it definitely falls in line with Paul Harris' 'State of Astonishment' theory (there's more on that in the Disappearance chapter, page 98–119). We watch transformations that are that impossibly fast precisely because we can't get our heads around them.

Above Sos & Victoria Petrosyan are four-times Guinness world-record breakers for the speed of their quick-change acts.

Overleaf To make the audience care about a transformation, you have to put it into the context of a narrative.

'The key to
all magic is
presentation'

VISUAL STARTING PISTOLS

I'll say it in this book a hundred times, but a lot of magic – especially stage illusion – is contextual. But to make a transformation contextual, it can be a good idea to make it part of a bigger routine – often you don't make it a stand-alone trick. To make somebody care about a transformation you have to put it into a narrative in some way, so that it means something. For example, after the intermission in my show and just as the second half of the show starts up, a dancer comes on stage. She's doing her thing, really beautifully, and then she covers herself with a large, red silk cloth and – BOOM – it's me. So I use a transformation as the way to get on stage for the second act – it acts like a kind of visual starting pistol for the second half. The key to all magic is presentation and to introduce nine kinds of illusion seamlessly into one performance or show takes real skill. You really have to focus on the through-line, the connections between one illusion and the next.

Another transformation would be right at the end of my Doves act. When I've finished producing the birds and have put them into the cage, I cover it with a black cloth. When I pull the cloth back, the cage has vanished and in place of the birds is an assistant. It's just part of a bigger illusion in this case, and felt like a perfect punchline when I did the act on *Britain's Got Talent*.

'The key to all magic is presentation...it takes real skill'

THE PSYCHOLOGY OF TRANSFORMATION

Transformation illusions fool us for a number of reasons. The first is the Midas aspect; simply that we want to believe this kind of magic is possible. This goodwill on the audience's part and the ability to engage our imagination at the expense of our good reason and common sense obviously helps the magician along.

It's worth unpicking why we like the idea of transformation. It's not unlike the cult of self-improvement; human beings are always striving to be better, healthier, thinner, smarter, quicker, and richer. We're so determined to find ways to make this happen that we sometimes often fall foul of solutions that seem to offer easy or cheap shortcuts (diets, superfoods, questionable alternative treatments). You've only got to look at the proliferation of cheap online banner adverts to know that we're suckers for a way to transform ourselves ('This housewife's $10 solution to a flatter stomach!'). In many ways it's rare to find someone who hasn't been suckered, at some point in their lives, into a too-good-to-be-true deal. Suspiciously cheap designer handbags or Nike trainers on eBay do sell, after all.

Above King Midas was given the power to turn anything he touched to gold, which fatally led to him turning his beloved daughter into a gold statue.

CHANGE BLINDNESS & TRANSFORMATION

From a psychological point of view, this willingness to believe ultimately affects how much we're able to focus on how transformations are done. It informs a kind of careless perception, where we're so focused on the end result (free money!) that we don't worry too much about how the magician gets there. What's interesting is that, even if you didn't care about money at all, it'd still be possible to switch objects right in front of you. And that's down to a theory called 'change blindness'.

In simple terms, change blindness is when we fail to notice significant changes to our environment. It's of interest to scientists because it proves our ability to conduct potentially dangerous everyday tasks – like driving – can be affected without us even realizing. Studying change blindness also helps scientists work out how much information we hold in our short-term visual memory from one moment to the next. And of course, it's of interest to magicians because, if objects or people can be swapped around without the audience knowing, it can help us design even better transformation illusions.

The idea of change blindness provides quite a big contrast with how we like to think about ourselves. We all assume we're aware of what's going on around us, that we're alert, perceptive individuals. 'Aware' is even used as a positive descriptor in lonely-hearts ads. But one 1998 experiment (that Derren Brown was able to reproduce successfully on his TV show) proves that's not the case. In the test, a stooge approaches a pedestrian to ask for directions. While he's giving them, a door is carried between the two people, giving the stooge time to swap places with someone else. When the door has passed, the pedestrian finishes off giving directions, completely unaware that it's not the person who initially approached him. Surprisingly, this switch or transformation worked 50 per cent of the time. Researchers came to the conclusion that, even if people did detect the switch, their brains weren't able to compute how that could happen. So in their brains, the image of the first stooge was simply overwritten by the image of the second. It's yet another example of how, when faced with information our

brains can't process or that doesn't 'fit', we find a way to rationalize, disregard, or erase it.

Later, scientists wanted to test how much of this 'not noticing' was down to the distraction (that is, the door), and how much might happen without it. Previously, it had been thought that change blindness occurred *because* of the distracting event. So they designed an experiment to see if people would notice a similar switch of people, even if nothing dramatic had happened.

In this 2002 Harvard experiment (which you can find quite easily on YouTube), participants enter an office where Man A, standing behind a counter, hands them a consent form to sign. Once it's signed, Man A takes back the form and ducks down behind the counter. But instead of Man A standing up, he switches with Man B, who stands up to give the participant an information pack. The participant is then sent into the next room where researchers could ask them questions. What's amazing is that this time the results were even more remarkable – 75 per cent of participants failed to notice that they were talking to an entirely different person. What's

especially odd is that participants were able to recall lots of other details about the scene – the sign above the man's head, what items were on the countertop. But not that the man had changed.

What this proves, of course, is that our brains can easily miss very important information even if there hasn't been a distraction to temporarily confuse us. So if the circumstances are right, it's possible to trick you halfway through a performance or illusion, and I don't even need loud bangs or distracting pyrotechnics to make that happen.

MISDIRECTION & OFF-BEATS

Sometimes when you see a close-up card trick, it'll seem as if it's gone wrong. Say I set up a simple trick in which you pick a card, don't show it to me, and then I have to find your card in the deck. In some tricks, I'll deliberately find the wrong card, because it'll produce an 'off-beat'. What I mean by this is that, even though it'll seem like the trick's gone bad, when I turn the 'wrong card' into the one you picked, I'll have a lovely and surprising transformation. As well as that, what happens during the off-beat just helps me fool you.

In an off-beat, lots of things are happening at once. In this example, there's disappointment (for you), perceived embarrassment (for me), and confusion (for everyone), because I wasn't able to find your card. What all of these elements lead to is a break in the audience's concentration. The fact that you have expectations (I will find your card) and that I've dashed them (by not finding it) makes you emotional. And we already know (from the Transposition chapter, see pages 34–57) that being emotional throws off your judgement.

Magic actually often happens in the off-beat – when people are busy recovering from one illusion and another starts, say, or when the audience is gasping. Sometimes you can produce an off-beat just by shuffling the pack and looking as if you're getting things ready. You also need to remember that, when

anything exciting happens, your natural instinct is to look at one another (and away from the stage) in order to share the moment with your family or friends. Comedy is also a great distraction for off-beats, and you may have experienced something like this yourself. Watching your favourite TV sitcom on your own, versus sharing it with friends, is a very different experience – but the best sitcoms benefit from repeat viewings because you miss some of the jokes the first time around. A good magician can harness the lack of concentration that results from all these off-beats, and build them into his or her performance.

DIRECTING THE AUDIENCE

Making people oblivious to what's right in front of them can also be a lot of fun. You can even do it in close-up situations – misdirection doesn't always rely on pyrotechnics, or smoke and mirrors. By simple virtue of where your attention is being focused, I can make you miss things. If I'm sitting close in front of you and I say, 'Watch the pen, don't take your eyes off the pen,' it's very possible that you physically and psychologically won't see me steal your cup of coffee. What's funny about this is that, even if you do realize you're being manipulated, it actually takes quite a long time for you to think, 'Hang on, why am I blindly following this guy's instructions?' The point is that I don't need very long to make my move, so even though it might be seconds, this will be enough time – or enough 'magic time' – to fool you.

Don't forget that magic is about tension and release – it relies on feelings and intuition, not facts. So maybe something very small like me walking across the stage can be a moment of tension or can build more tension, especially if I'm not speaking. If I'm silent, it's also easier to focus your attention on something specific and small. Then, as soon as I start speaking or making grand arm or hand gestures, you're going to be processing more images and that splits your attention. If you're a good magician, you'll be able to split or focus the attention of the audience, depending on what you need to achieve or hide.

'Magic is about tension and release – it relies on feelings and intuition, not facts'

Opposite Stand-up comedy, like magic, relies on taking advantage of the 'off-beat'. Chris Rock is a master of the art.

TEMPORAL ILLUSIONS

Because transformation is one of the forms of magic in which time is key, it's worth thinking about how subjective and changeable our perception of time can be. An easy way to demonstrate this is for you to try to count out ten seconds exactly, without looking at your phone or watch. How close to a 'real' ten seconds did you get? In reality, most of us have a very vague grasp of time passing, so how slow or fast we think a day or year is going can depend on what we're doing (think about the last time you had a terrible day at work. You know when you 'clock watch' that time goes slower than ever). There's even evidence to suggest that the reason we feel time passing faster as we get older, is down to us having fewer new experiences. When you're a kid, you're constantly doing new things, and it's as if your brain was making a new 'page' for each one (this may be why the summer holidays felt like they stretched on forever). It's also like when you go away for a weekend and do lots of different

Right A good magician can affect the audience's perception of time.

activities or go to many new places. Those couple of days away from your routine can feel much, much longer.

The same thing can be true for how we perceive time during a magician's performance. Without wanting to sound too pretentious, time can become quite elastic and good magicians can affect the audience's perception of time by making small alterations to their performance. Even on a stage in front of 2,000 people, it's possible for me to be either ahead of or behind you. This means that you can be under the impression that an illusion has just begun, even though I've actually already done it.

The longer you've been doing magic, the easier it is to access this time-altering skill. After a while, you instinctively begin to understand that if you stand somewhere long enough or if you look in one particular direction then the audience will too. You start to get a feel for the shift in the tension in the room, and this allows you to arrest or move a situation on by changing your own pace. You can also manipulate the audience's sense of when a trick has 'begun' or 'ended' through sensory cues like lights, narration, and music. David Blaine is incredible when he performs at his own, unique pace and the persona he's created as a magician (a bit odd, a bit quiet) allows him to be deliberately slow and unusual in his behaviour. This is smart because it creates tension. So when he pulls off a trick, it's even more impressive. Ultimately, it's your job as a magician to build anticipation and there are plenty of simple, non-verbal ways to do this.

PERFORMANCE & TENSION

On stage, all this means that you have to move, speak, look, and walk in ways that are not necessarily natural, so you can alter the pace of the performance. Strangely, the audience doesn't question it, partly because a lot of people expect you to be showy or 'weird' and also because it's probably what people have come to expect from magicians (this is one of the only occasions when people's prior knowledge of – or clichés about – magicians come in handy). We walk around the stage when we don't necessarily need to, we move away from our props to let you inspect them. And in the end, of course, it's totally worth it because when you hear people gasp, it makes you feel incredible. It's not a question of faking it, either, because you do need to feel that tension along with the audience. If you don't, performances can seem unbalanced somehow, because the audience and you aren't having a shared experience.

Magic is also much more powerful if you try to perform each illusion as if it's the first time you've done it (even if you've done it many times). Doing a death-defying escape for the 50,000th time might not feel dangerous to you, but the audience needs and deserves to feel the danger. So you access the part of your brain that remembers when you were scared (it's a bit like method acting, I guess). I really need and like to feel that danger, even if I've been in training for months and am in really good shape. For me, if you get too comfortable, you might miss a cue or perform the illusion wrong. And then you could really hurt yourself. Funnily enough, this even applies to doing close-up card tricks. Part of my brain needs to believe that the card is in Place A, even though I've already moved it to Place B. In my mind, for that brief moment, I have to look at my hands and see the cards as you would. Because if it shows on my face and in my voice, you'll believe it too.

Opposite So much of the success of a magic trick is in the power of the performance.

illusion

NOW YOU SEE ME...

DISAPPEARANCE ACTS

WHAT IS DISAPPEARANCE?

Disappearance is almost like a kicker to a lot of magic, or a precursor to an effect. Generally speaking, to make something disappear won't be as powerful as if you made it disappear and reappear – these illusions rarely happen in isolation. So disappearances are often used in addition to another form of magic. With my Levitation illusion (a homage to Le Roy's) the disappearance of the floating person is a punchline to that act. The levitation is further enhanced by ending in a disappearance.

This goes back to the idea of magic needing to have a narrative, so the audience experiences that tension and release. If you just vanish something, it can often feel inconclusive or unfinished. For example, if I am on stage and I vanish, it's cool, but the audience wants closure, they need you to come back. The exception to this rule is when you've got an object of excessive size. So if I was to vanish a tank, nobody would really care whether I re-produced it or not. The size and the impossibility of the vanish would 'sell' the illusion by itself.

FAKE FINGERS

There's some disagreement over who first invented it, but people all over the world have seen magical disappearances achieved using a 'thumb tip'. It's a small fake tip of the thumb, which tends to be made out of flesh-coloured rubber. The idea is that you can stuff things (like silk scarves) into the thumb tip, which can be concealed in your hand. Then when you put the tip over your real thumb – hey presto! – the scarves have vanished. I hesitate to give that kind of disappearance trick away, but it's the kind of thing that comes in kids' magic kits. I had one in the first kit I got, along with a mini cups-and-balls routine and a tiny drawer you could hide coins in.

The first time I was paid to perform a disappearance routine, it was for a kid's birthday party in a McDonald's. It didn't go very

'If you vanish, the audience wants closure, they need you to come back'

well at all – partly because I was 12 years old and partly because, for some strange reason, I had decided to wear a clown suit. The party was just in the corner – it wasn't even in a separate room or anything – so everyone walking into McDonald's could see me die 'on stage'. I also had a trick with silk scarves – two blue and one yellow – and I didn't even know what you were supposed to do with them. So I just put the yellow one and the blue one into the velvet bag and then pulled them out and – Ta da! – they were tied together. I think the audience were just confused; I mean, I bombed, man, it was really lame. My act was only four minutes because I just did all the tricks I knew in double-quick time, all rushed because I was nervous. I think my parents just wondered when I was going to grow out of it, but of course I never did.

Enough memories, though. The thumb tip – however common – is still interesting from a psychological point of view. The thing is, most people only know the thumb tip as 'that gimmick you use to do the old-fashioned scarves routine'. This means that if you make money vanish or disappear a cigarette, they don't immediately think 'Ooh, thumb tip'. This should tell you that even when people know the 'answers', they rarely apply them in the right way or at the right time. People will file magic secrets in their brains along with the routine in which they saw them used – so they aren't thinking about that secret or recalling that information when the same method is used for a completely different illusion. Clever…

Above You can stuff things like silk scarves into a thumb tip.

THE ELEPHANT VANISHES

If you wanted to guarantee a full house at the turn of the 20th century, you would make something disappear. Alongside magic and cabaret, there was a huge public interest in science and the paranormal, so vanishing illusions often played side by side with, or were part of, popular science lectures or séances. One famous act was called Pepper's Ghost. It thrilled audiences at the Royal Polytechnic Institute in London and was devised by a lecturer and professor called John Henry Pepper, who used a combination of light, secret mirrors, and hidden projectors to show a ghost appearing and disappearing onstage. So little was known about theatrical or scientific special effects back then, so magic, science, and the supernatural occupied the same space in the public imagination. You can see why audiences at the time found these subjects so enthralling – science really was magical, because it was so new. There's actually a fantastic Arthur C Clarke quote about this: 'Any sufficiently advanced technology is indistinguishable from magic.' Mirrors and projectors were advanced technologies and that's why they were magic.

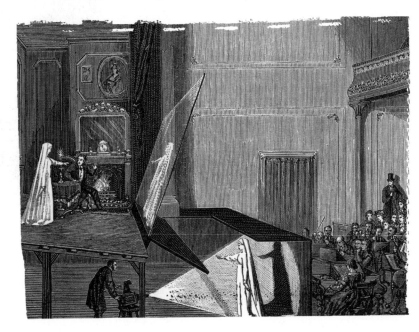

Right 'Pepper's Ghost' was an illusion devised by John Henry Pepper, which was performed in front of audiences at the Royal Polytechnic Institute.

For Houdini, the most dramatic thing to vanish was an elephant. Huge, frightening, and imposing, elephants couldn't be seen on television or on phones or computers, as they are today. They represented something powerful and deeply exotic. This gave the illusion another dimension and allowed illusionists to use a 'show and tell' narration ('the animal is THIS big and THIS heavy and comes from THIS far away') as a way of making their show more impressive. If it was THAT heavy, how could the animal be moved quickly? If it was THAT wild, how could it be trained? If it was THAT big, how could it be hidden?

Houdini was smart; he made sure to present the illusion in such a way that he could deal with his detractors and eliminate possible methods for the audience. His elephant (called Jennie and wearing a huge blue ribbon) was ushered into a large wooden box that sat on top of castors, thereby eliminating the use of a trapdoor. But he also made sure to place the box right in the middle of the stage, so it would have been impossible to move the elephant out through the back. Some reports talk about a brightly lit stage, which would have given Houdini nowhere to hide. However it was done, it managed to fool both the audience and Houdini's rivals, thereby guaranteeing more press. When he was asked to reveal how he did it, he just said, 'Even the elephant doesn't know.'

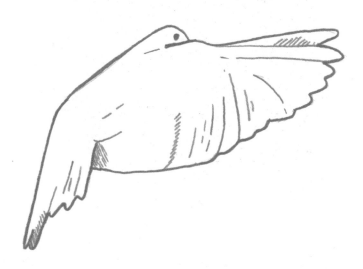

Opposite Houdini and his elephant, Jennie, whom he made disappear in front of an astounded audience.

THE SQUISHER

'I'm still surprised what people will agree to when you put them under pressure, it's a weird power to have'

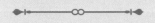

When I performed a vanishing trick for my special on British television, I wanted to involve the audience in some way. When you reach out, you're making a link and I like to do that, to decrease the distance between me and my audience. I want them to be closer to what's happening. So I borrowed a red plaid shirt from this guy Rob, who was nice enough to take it off and sit in his seat topless for the whole act. Presenter Christine Bleakley asked him to do it, and the camera was right on him, so I guess he couldn't say no (your inability to say no to a magician is something we actually use against you in card tricks and mind-reading acts, but we'll get to that later). I'm still surprised what people will agree to when you put them under pressure, it's a weird power to have.

The first thing I do is to show the audience my table frame, which can slide around on castors so you can see it from all angles. It's hollow and made of steel so the lights pick it out. Then, as two of my assistants put the tabletop on, I'm saying; 'We're going to assemble everything in front of you, so you can see all sides at all times, so you know we're not cheating.' I get the audience to welcome one of my dancers, Lola, on stage, and she puts on the guy's shirt over her little black dress and hops onto the table which is spun around for a second time. Then two of my male assistants bring over both sides of The Squisher, which are fixed to the table – they look kind of like book ends, with metal sides. Lola's right between the two ends, her long legs stretched out. Then an assistant and I pull screens across so Lola is hidden, and we push the two ends of The Squisher together. Right together, fast. Lola should be squished inside but she's vanished. All that's left is Rob's red plaid shirt. We push the table to the back of the stage, where it stays.

That should be the end, but I think you need some resolution. So we pull another table (this one is square) from the back of the stage and twirl it around so you can see it's just regular. Well, regular apart from the frame above it, which lets you pull up a

Opposite Georges Méliès was a French filmmaker and magician, who experimented with special effects illusions on screen.

GEORGES MÉLIÈS

Moving pictures must have seemed magical in themselves back in the early days of cinema, but Georges Méliès (1861–1938) went one step further, experimenting with the special effects that the medium of film allowed as a way to create illusions. He discovered his 'stop trick' by accident when his camera mechanism jammed – the camera stopped filming and when it picked up again where it had left off once he had fixed it, it appeared as though the scene had changed in a split second rather than proceeding in real time. Méliès made use of this technique for his disappearance tricks: he would film a magician making an 'abracadabra!' gesture and then stop the camera. The magician's assistant would then move out of shot, so that when Méliès started the camera again it would look as if the she had disappeared when the magician made his gesture.

curtain that goes right around the frame, kind of like a curtain on a shower cubicle. The curtain is pulled up about 6 feet, and I toss the red shirt over the curtain as the boys pull it up. But just as soon as it's up, they're lowering it again. And standing there is Lola, wearing the red shirt. At which point, I think it's time Rob got his shirt back.

THE BRAIN & DISAPPEARANCE

We can all probably think of someone or something we would like to disappear. The idea's pretty potent; with a click of your fingers, you could just make it all go away. Those feelings don't always come from a good place but they are quite human, so it's easy to see why people like the idea of disappearance illusions. It's all so neat, quick, and final. Are you thinking of someone you'd like to make disappear right now? Of course you are.

In terms of magic, though, it can be quite a challenge. For obvious reasons, if you're working with large, live, wild animals you need to do a lot of planning. Animal welfare and an experienced theatrical team are very important. Meanwhile, making smaller objects disappear – though it seems much easier from a practical point of view – also throws up its own challenges. When you're working the room as a working magician, or just doing tricks for your friends, you know their eyes are going to be *everywhere*, so you have to be super slick. You'll also have seen many magicians wearing suit jackets even though they don't really look like the kinds of dudes who would wear suits every day. The fact is, that some tricks require a sleeve and making your suit look 'natural' can be kind of tricky (I don't wear suits often in real life, so I figured it would be weird if I did it on stage). Similarly, in the spirit of proving they're honest, some magicians will make a big show of rolling up their sleeves. We're not stupid; we know it's the first place you'd look.

Opposite A poster for John Nevil Maskelyne's show at London's Egyptian Hall. His background in clockmaking helped with the detail required for close-up illusions.

EGYPTIAN HALL

ENGLAND'S HOME OF MYSTERY.
PERFORMANCES DAILY AT THREE AND EIGHT

TRAPPED BY MAGIC.

Mr. Maskelyne's latest illusory sketch, introducing the most astounding mysteries ever witnessed, in one of which a performer rises into space in full light, and a solid steel hoop, which is examined by the audience before and after it is used, is passed completely over him from head to foot.

The "Daily Telegraph" says: "Mr. Maskelyne has surpassed himself. . . . . The tricks ought to astonish scientific London."

"The Standard" says: "The illusions are without parallel."

"A Dainty Dish to set before a King."

WHAT'S YOUR MOTIVATION?

So to make close-up disappearances look good, you've got to practise. Practise, practise, practise. Magicians are like swans – all the work is happening right out of view – so you need to be quick, deft, and natural in your movements. This means you'll inevitably be spending hours, days, months – often *years* – practising and mastering moves and sleights again and again. Your motivation is how amazing it's going to look when you've got it down perfect, and when that doesn't keep you going, you have to develop (if you don't naturally have one already) a fascination for how tricks work. If you have that, then it can still be satisfying to perform a trick for the hundredth time. I was, and still am, obsessed with it all, because I think there's an elegance to a lot of magic. I also love the heritage of it, that someone thought about the quickest, most efficient, and most invisible way to move card A to position B, and that you get to apply the results of all their hard work. The mechanics are fascinating when you understand them, and if you want to be great you have to turn your body into a machine of deception.

People sometimes wonder if the secrets of magic – when you find them out – are a disappointment. I would say no. When something's really well engineered, it's not mundane; there's a genius to it. And there are lots of incredible magicians from throughout history who had the ability to apply hidden engineering for the benefit of the audience's happiness. Robert-Houdin and John Nevil Maskelyne – rightly held up as masters of magic – both had a background in clockmaking. They understood how to make something sweeping and beautiful, like a watch face, by manipulating and assembling a series of tiny cogs and movements. There's selflessness and a beauty to that kind of work, I think, because all the really tricky stuff is hidden behind the face of the watch. Robert-Houdin even invented a 'mystery clock' where the hands float on the clock face and where there's no visible connection to the workings at all. They often have a glass or crystal (that is, transparent) face and the hands of the clock just appear to swoop around, displaying the time, when all the mechanics are hidden. I guess that's as good a metaphor for magic as any.

Above Robert-Houdin's 'mystery clock', with hands that float on the clock face.

Opposite Harry Houdini was inspired by Jean-Eugène Robert-Houdin, even to the point of borrowing his name.

Overleaf I made controversial TV presenter Jeremy Kyle disappear – which proved popular with the audience!

HOUDIN'S MYSTERY CLOCK

Jean-Eugène Robert-Houdin (1805–1871), the man who would go on to inspire Harry Houdini's stage name, was a clockmaker as well as a magician. He combined his two passions to make 'mystery clocks', with hands that appear to float over a transparent dial and with seemingly no mechanism, leaving the viewer to wonder exactly how such a device tells the time.

His solutions to the 'mystery movement' behind these clocks were ingenious, mainly involving hiding the mechanism in the clock base and attaching the hands to a second transparent dial that rotated behind the one that was visible. The second dial was turned by attachments hidden inside the clock frame, an example of a feat of engineering so clever it seems like magic.

Sometimes I'm asked if a natural ability to engineer things – especially on stage where you have large, complicated props – is something magicians have in common. I don't think it is, but I do wonder if a lot of us are inherently good at reverse-engineering, because we're constantly trying to find out how things work and pushing at the boundaries of what's possible. I think you also get into the habit of re-appropriation – taking ordinary objects and finding a way to use them in magic. Let's take something like a retractable key chain. You see them everywhere, hung from skaters' belt loops, on the key ring of a security guard. But when magicians see one, we don't see a retractable key chain. We're examining the possibility that we could use it somehow in one of our illusions, to remove an object quickly. Your brain starts whirring, 'Let's turn that into something that vanishes things!' When you've been in magic a long time, you realize that you're constantly looking for new and novel ways to apply existing technology. It sounds crazy, but I feel the same way about glue, posterboard, tape, and rubber cement. Basically an office supply store is a magician's heaven. You can build an entire show out of those stores.

THE STATE OF ASTONISHMENT

What happens to human beings when they see fireworks? You've been there yourself, I'm sure, alongside your family or your friends, and suddenly the noises start. Grown men and women start making 'Ooh' noises and gasping. Fireworks make us act like children – spellbound by spectacle and wonder. We do it without even thinking and it's a great leveller. It reminds me what a great capacity for awe we have. It seems almost instinctive, even if we think of ourselves as quite cynical.

This childlike wonder and surprise are ultimately what every magician wants to produce

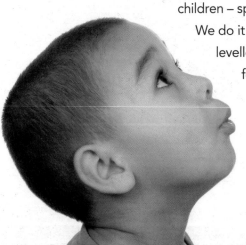

in an audience. That's the golden ideal and it's so perfect when you see it – jaded old guys who suddenly gasp, giggles from tired mothers who've seen it all before. When you can provoke that in people, it's a real gift and a privilege. It's the key to why people like me get obsessed with magic and why we're so happy to turn it into a career. But why are there so few moments of wonder in our everyday lives?

Paul Harris is an inventor, magician, and writer and in magic circles, he's kind of a legend. He has a theory about childlike wonder in an incredible essay called 'Astonishment is Our Natural State of Mind.' It's a beautiful piece of writing that argues that when we see things we can't explain we're actually being returned to 'a clear primal state of mind' – so not childhood, not naivety, just our natural state. You should read the whole thing if you can find it, but here's my favourite part:

'You come into the world a blank slate. No ideas about who you are or what anything is. You're just being. And it all feels great… because there are no options, or opinions, or judgements. There is no right or wrong. Everything is everything. That's what you see in a baby's eyes. Pure child's mind. Then, very quickly, we learn stuff. The names of 10,000 things, who we are, what we're supposed to be, what's good and bad according to the current rules of the game. And you organize all of this information into little boxes. And when any new information comes along you file it in the appropriate box.

'…There's no particular reality to any of this. But it's in your head and you know the territory and it's where all of your thoughts do their thinking. But we quickly forget what was there in the first place because these thousands of little thought-boxes are stacked up so tight that the original clear space of child's mind is completely covered up. It's not gone. It's just blocked by this wall of over-stuffed boxes.

'And then along comes a focused piece of strange in the form of a magical effect. Let's say this book vanishes from your hands. "Poof" no book. Your trained mind races into action and tries to put the piece of strange into one of its rational boxes. But no box will

'When you can provoke this childlike wonder and surprise in people, it's a real gift and a privilege'

Opposite All magicians want to produce a state of childlike wonder in their audience.

hold it. *At that moment of trying to box the unboxable your world-view breaks up. The boxes are gone. And what's left? Simply what was always there. Your natural state of mind. That's the moment of astonishment.* The sudden experience of going from boxes to no boxes.'

You can see how motivating this essay might be when you're trying to learn for hours how to palm (vanish) a coin, can't you? What it also does for me is to legitimize and give credit to a feeling that people often dismiss as 'silly' – it's like being wowed by stuff that isn't cool. But I think sometimes in life you don't need an explanation; you can just revel in the feeling that maybe you don't know everything, and can't explain everything, and that's okay. It's also worth remembering that what Harris describes in his essay has kind of been proven by all the psychological and neurological studies that have been done about how we watch magic. Magic puts the pause button on our brains and our lives and that's why we do it.

FILLING IN THE GAPS

Science calls those brain pauses cognitive dissonance. I've mentioned cognitive dissonance quite a lot in this book, but with good reason. It's because our brains often fail us. It's not that our eyes aren't seeing, or that we can't hear the music blaring from the theatre speakers, or smell the dry ice. It's just that what we see is being processed wrong, allowing us to draw false conclusions.

A good example of this inability to really see is drawing. We can all think of someone in our school art class who was amazing at drawing, a real natural. Why do you think that was? I think it's because people who can really capture what something looks like have been born with (or are able to cultivate) an ability to look at things in an unfiltered, unprocessed kind of way. Natural illustrators see in light and shade, rather than drawing big black outlines around each object.

They take things at face value, without trying to draw too many conclusions or make too many assumptions.

The thing is, most people can't see things without subconsciously making assumptions or filling in those gaps. It's how our brains process visual information and then tell us what we're seeing. And when you vanish things, this assumption-making really helps. A good example would be the French Drop.

Without giving too much away, a French Drop is a very common, basic move that magicians can use to vanish objects. I might use it if I was trying to make a coin disappear, taking the coin from my left hand and sweeping my right hand up and out to the side so you can see it. When I open my right hand the coin is gone, but you've clearly seen me take it from my left hand. So where is it? To give you a clue, the French Drop is used when you want to vanish something before the audience knows it's gone. I need you to believe that I still have it (in my right hand) and I won't just use my hands to sell this assumption to you. I'll use my eyes and my body language so that everything I do says 'he took the coin from his left hand and put it in his right'. This will make your brain fill in the gaps – from me picking it up and sweeping it to the side until you're absolutely sure it's still in my right hand. Absolutely sure that is, until I show you my empty right palm.

Above The French Drop is a basic coin trick most magicians know and use.

Opposite Being able to draw is a matter of being able to see things in an unfiltered way.

The French Drop is interesting to neuroscientists and psychologists because it can demonstrate how skilled magicians can affect how we process visual and aural information and come to the wrong psychological conclusions. So in April 2015, scientists Flip Phillips, Michael B Natter and Eric J L Egan decided to put the French Drop to the test, by asking both skilled and unskilled magicians to perform the move. They put their performances on videotape, asking the magicians to do one 'drop' where the coin was transferred to the right hand and one where it remained hidden in the left. All the spectators had to do was work out what hand the coin ended up in. Then the scientists could analyse the perceptions of the spectators using fMRI technology, thereby working out if the magicians were able to exercise what scientists call 'attentional control' (and what magicians call misdirection). Could the spectators tell when the coin was passed from hand to hand? Did they know when it was done? According to the study:

'Attentional control can arise from a variety of sources, ranging from overt social cues ("Hey! Look over there!") to subtle, practised, and precise perceptual-motor manipulations. Thus, magic can help us disentwine how the performance of the action contributes to the perception of that action.'

What the study found was probably unsurprising to most magicians, but also kind of reassuring. First of all, by measuring the subtle muscle movements and trajectory of the magicians' hands, they were able to tell how much more successfully the deception was achieved by the skilled magicians (like I say, you gotta practise!). But more interesting was that they were able to find out from spectators when they thought the deception had taken place. And when the skilled magicians performed, they nearly always got it wrong.

'Most people can't see things without subconsciously making assumptions'

AS GOOD AS NEW

---∞---

THE MAGIC OF RESTORATION

WHAT IS A RESTORATION ILLUSION?

Restoration illusions – like many kinds of magic – also play into that God-like idea that a magician can mend the unmendable and fix the unfixable. If you had superpowers this is one of the skills you'd want to have, alongside being able to make things appear, flying, and being able to see inside people's minds. We've all been clumsy and broken something important to us – and it makes you so mad; there's a moment of disbelief when you look at the shattered pieces of say, your mum's favourite vase – or felt that fast, sinking feeling when you realize you've spilt coffee on an important photograph. Having the ability to restore order in horrible situations like this can make restoration illusions the most fun tricks to perform. And maybe it's an ego thing, but people tend to be really blown away by restoration magic, especially close up.

In the structure of any show, though, you need have to have a reason for something to be restored. This is that idea about context again and why it's so important that the illusions you perform make some kind of sense; why it helps if they're part of a 'story'. So, even if you can restore something, there has to be a reason why it was broken in the first place – you don't just come on stage and start smashing stuff up. One way to achieve this is to make it look as if the initial break was a mistake and not part of your routine at all. Then, the audience is shocked; they assume it wasn't meant to happen. That way it's all the more satisfying for them when you magically make things all right again.

Right It's best not to try the restoration trick of tearing up money until you've had a lot of practice!

DESTROY AT WILL

There are lots of ways to break and mend things in a close-up environment. You can take a £20 note from someone, rip it up right in their face and then magically unfold it to show it's still intact. You can borrow a watch from someone in your audience, place it a bag and smash it with a hammer, telling them you're just checking to see if it's 'shock resistant'. I don't recommend you try any of these, of course, until you've had some practice…

The problem is that these kinds of tricks still fall into the 'no-narrative' category for me. I prefer it if there's a reason – however crazy – for the 'breaking' part of a restoration illusion. Michael Carbonaro's restoration tricks are a great example. He's a magician who combines magic with pranking members of the public – he has a whole TV show, *The Carbonaro Effect*, where they put him in different situations and film the reactions of the public with hidden cameras. In one, he's pretending to work at a carwash, so he's greeting customers, telling them where to park up, what the service involves, that kind of thing. An older guy pulls up, and Michael is all sunshine – big smiles, how's-your-day-sir – before pointing out that the guy's car has a little scratch on the driver-side window. 'Can you see through that ok? Because we want you to be driving safely,' Carbonaro says. 'We'll fix that right up for you.' Then he points out where the guy needs to go and pay. While the man is speaking to the sales rep, Michael takes out a huge wrench and smashes the scratched car window. There's a huge noise, glass flies everywhere. But Carbonaro plays it cool. 'All right, sir, I got this one all taken out for you, okay?' he says.

'You've taken what out?' says the man, looking worried. 'You've done what? What did you do to my window?' But Carbonaro acts like it's no problem, nothing shakes him. 'Well I showed you there

Above Michael Carbonaro combines magic with pranking members of the public.

was a scratch on it,' he explains, smiling. 'Why did you break my window?' says the man, rattled. 'Oh, I just smashed out the *dealer window* so you'll be able to see better. Has nobody told you that yet?' The man looks mystified. Dealer windows? What the hell are they? But then Carbonaro takes out the remaining shards of glass from the frame, calmly opens the door and winds up the window. And there it is – a completely new window, rising up in the door, as if it had been there the whole time. 'All you do is just smash out the dealer window, and roll up the real one,' says Carbonaro with a totally straight face, pointing to the car door. 'And there's three more in here,' he says, tapping on the side of the door.

This is a flawless restoration illusion because it ticks all the criteria. Context? They're in a real-world situation, a place that nobody suspects is part of a TV show. Motivation? Carbonaro is 'mending' the scratched window, he's just cleared it with the guy. Explanation? He's just taking out the 'dealer window'. So in this illusion, it doesn't matter that the explanation is crazy, or that dealer windows don't exist. When you give people a reason for the magic, they believe it. And I think that's beautiful.

One of my other favourite memories of a restoration was when David Copperfield did a tear-and-restore trick with a priceless baseball card. It belonged to Wayne Gretzky, who was a very

'Being able to restore order in horrible situations makes restoration illusions fun to perform'

Overleaf We magicians know that people enjoy watching shocking things as entertainment.

famous professional ice hockey player. I guess it was the prized item in his collection, the sort of thing he would run back into his burning house to retrieve. This tiny piece of cardboard was hugely rare – it had a picture of Honus Wagner (a very famous baseball player) on it and it was also signed by him. At the time, in 1993, it was worth $500,000, but a similar card fetched $2.8 million at auction in 2010. Basically, it's an insanely valuable thing.

So, Copperfield meets Gretzky in a TV studio and asks to see the card, which is kept in a special Perspex case so it can't get damaged. He talks to Gretzky about how rare it is. And then – very slowly and deliberately – he tears it up, right in front of him. I remember watching this as a tiny kid and looking at Gretzky's face, because he was obviously horrified even though he knows what Copperfield does; he would have seen his TV specials before. But there's something so awful, and strangely watchable, when something so highly prized, like this tiny piece of baseball memorabilia, is being utterly ruined. We feel like rubberneckers. But we can't look away.

Then, just as slowly as he's ripped it, Copperfield manages to put the card back together in his hands, rubbing his fingers over the rips until they're not there anymore. And this was stunning to me; because of how slowly he did it, because it made it all the more magical. Now, obviously, a restoration like this doesn't have the same context or narrative as the other tricks above. But at the same time, Copperfield wasn't just ripping it up and then – bang! FLASH! – it's back together. He made a big, long production of it. And what that taught me is that when something doesn't belong to you, but you get to see it destroyed, you get to live vicariously through the person who the trick is being done to. The audience is so invested in it, so the magician has to make the most of that and take their time. In fact, all good restoration magic should make the audience feel this way.

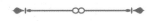

'Cutting live animals or people up has always had a fantastically bloodthirsty side to it'

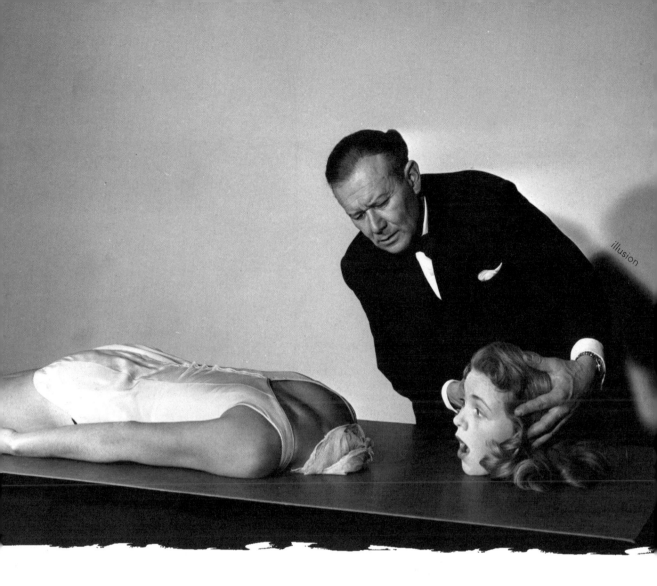

illusion

RESTORATION MAGIC THROUGHOUT HISTORY

There are descriptions of restoration magic as far back as 2600BC, when an Egyptian magician called Dedi was told to appear before King Cheops, the man responsible for the pyramids at Giza. Dedi was a master of restoration and specialized in rather macabre tricks involving animals. He would chop off the head of a goose, duck, or ox and then restore it. King Cheops – clearly a bit eager for blood, or maybe just a natural Vegas showman with a taste for one-

Above That's one obvious thing about restoration tricks: they're not something you can really freestyle.

upmanship – wanted Dedi to go one better, and chop off the head of a prisoner. Luckily Dedi refused. That's one obvious thing about restoration magic – it's not something you can really freestyle.

But cutting live animals or people up has always had a fantastically bloodthirsty side to it. We've all seen illusions in which a magician cuts a lady in half or puts her in box or crate, only to thrust swords through it. There's something about being shocked that humans are entertained by. For me, the classic Sawing A Lady In Half is performed by Penn & Teller, because their spin on this restoration illusion is so gruesome and bloody.

Penn & Teller use two of our darkest desires against us here – not only do they claim to reveal how the trick is done (thereby satisfying our curiosity), they also make sure that the trick itself is spectacularly grisly (thereby satisfying our bloodlust). This is not an accident, very little in magic is. Penn & Teller also frame their explanation/performance beautifully. They begin by talking about alternative medicine and how so much of it is based on the placebo principle; as Penn says, 'You want it to work, so you believe it does.' This is clever because it shows how well Penn & Teller know their audience. People watch and admire them, not only because they are fantastic at magic, but because they make it clear that they're on the side of regular people – they're not going to stand by and let you be exploited by scammers, hoaxers, or swindlers. Penn & Teller are smart, sceptical, modern people. We hope that by watching them, some of that clever will rub off on us, too.

So the lady gets into the long box and her head pokes out one end and her feet the other. A huge saw begins to turn round – fast – as Penn reassures the assistant that 'This is going to feel great.' They say they're doing it to 'realign her chakras'. Then they bring down the saw and it starts to tear into the wooden box – splinters are flying off the table – but the lady is smiling. And that's where I need to point out that the fixed, cheesy grins of magicians'

Opposite Penn & Teller make sure their tricks are spectacularly grisly.

assistants are no accident. They're meant to reassure the part of your brain that is trying to process what looks a lot like a murder.

Penn & Teller bring the saw back up and pull the two halves of box containing the woman apart – suddenly there's a strange gap between her torso and her legs – just as we expect, because we've seen the trick before. Except this time, they don't stop there. First, they reveal that actually, the woman's middle is merely hidden down in the recesses of the (gimmicked) table and she can't be harmed because there's a steel plate covering her abdomen. Then they explain that, even if the steel plate were removed, it wouldn't matter, because there's a steel pin that stops the saw from going too far down. The only trouble is, Teller's just removed the pin. And now the saw is driving it's way through the woman's middle. She's screaming and a huge stripe of blood is painted on the wall behind Penn & Teller, who pull the table fully apart this time, seemingly spilling the guts of the beautiful assistant all over the floor.

Opposite Spend too much time around magicians and you might lose your head.

RESTORATION

Whether it's Wolverine recovering from grave injuries with astonishing speed, or Superman flying around the world so fast that he can travel back in time to prevent Lois Lane from dying, in the world of superheroes it's perfectly plausible for things to be fixed quickly and effortlessly. Back in the land of everyday mortals, we might at best be able to resort to superglue or stitches, if there is a chance of mending something at all.

But when it comes to tricky situations like bringing people back from the dead or restoring a priceless ruined object so that it's as good as new, superhuman skills are required, far beyond normal human capabilities. And it's even better if it's done with a bit of flash.

BURNING THE CANDLE

I've worked on various restoration illusions, and it's hard to find one that's not too cheesy or overdone. Seeing someone being sawn in half on stage is always compelling, because if it were real, this act would be horrifying. Because you know the person is not really being cut in half, however, there's a weird fascination in seeing it happen right in front of your eyes: you feel squeamish while also knowing that there's nothing to be squeamish about.

I enjoy some of the more shocking restoration tricks, but there's also one I like because it's a pretty 'quiet' illusion: just me, sitting on the edge of the stage, close up with the audience; there are no flashing lights, no life-endangering moments, just straight-up magic.

This illusion does involve a little spark of danger I guess, as the trick sees me holding a piece of string over a lit candle (don't try this at home!). The candle burns its way through the string, of course, leaving it in two pieces. I make sure to show the audience

Above Sawing a beautiful assistant in half is a popular trick around the world.

the separate pieces of string. Next, I take a longer piece of string and hold that over the candle. Again, the flame burns through the string, making it come apart in two pieces.

To build up the intrigue (the audience is wondering what I'm doing by this point), I keep repeating this with more lengths of string. Then, once I have a few of them, I ball all the small pieces of string into my fist and rub my hands together. When I open my hands, the audience sees that I am holding a single, restored piece of string. Like I say, it's not a big, showy illusion, but it has the right mix of simplicity and mystery to hold an audience's attention.

THE ALLURE OF THE MACABRE

When you think about the audience for a restoration trick, you have to obey a few rules. First off, we go back again to the narrative idea, and how it's important for every story to have an element of resolution. Every week in your favourite television shows, the characters resolve something, learn something, or find something out. This idea – that 'order has been restored' – is very pleasing to the human brain because our brains like patterns, they help us to file information.

Then, you've got the not altogether cutesy fact that people like to see nasty things. Horror movies are a case in point – the slasher movie is constantly being reinvented for new generations, and there are always countless films in production in which innocent, sexy teenagers get chased and destroyed by something evil. Even the storylines for horror movies are so well established as to be set in stone; total clichés. We know our heroine will go into the basement where the lights don't work. We know the floating camera angle won't let us see what's behind us. We all still love those jump-in-your-seat crashes and thumps, even when they're signposted by spooky music.

But even real-life atrocities have a peculiar attraction. When driving past a terrible traffic accident, people will slow down and stare, wanting to see what's happened. Part of this is primeval

'You've got the not altogether cutesy fact that people like to see nasty things'

– our prehistoric ancestors needed to confront danger in order to decide whether to fight or flee. Even at the less shocking end of the spectrum, we love to see people falling over or walking into things on YouTube and on television. Whether it's little kids getting a faceful of swing in a park or a wedding party falling into a swimming pool, it all gets shared on Facebook. We don't even question our impulse to do this. Why are we attracted to horrible things happening to others?

The truth is that it's always been this way. Pre-internet, radio, and television, it was normal to take your kids to watch the latest criminal or blasphemer meet his end at the guillotine, crucifix, or gallows. Magicians know we have it in our hearts to watch shocking things as entertainment and so it's only natural to include these elements in our shows. We'll look at this in detail in the Escapology chapter (see pages 164–189), but it's worth remembering that, however modern we become, our brains still betray us. We're all kind of nasty, and magic gives us the opportunity to face up to that fact in an innocent way. You know Penn & Teller aren't really sawing that lady in half and that's why people laugh when they watch the illusion. Yes, it's gross, but it's normal to find release in those moments. Laughter seems wrong in those moments, but it's really just the expression of relief.

EMOTIONAL INVESTMENT

Another powerful aspect of restoration – especially close up – is that magicians are able to use people's natural sense of protection over their own possessions against them. When you use objects that belong to your audience – maybe a watch given to them by a grandfather, or just their own, hard-earned money – you know they're going to pay attention. After all, a performer's worst nightmare is the crowd who can't be bothered to hang around and see how the trick ends; we wouldn't do magic to an empty room. It's also true that this emotional investment is scientifically proven to muddy our perceptions, and that's music to a magician's ears. Let's look at how.

THE ENDOWMENT EFFECT

Psychologists are fascinated by what they call the 'endowment effect'. This is the name for when people put a higher value on things they own, simply because they own them. There are many experiments that prove this phenomenon, including one from 1968 in which it was found that people who placed a bet on a horse gave it a better chance of winning after they'd placed their bet than before because the horse had changed from 'a good bet' to 'my bet'. But it's not only adults who are susceptible to these irrational valuations. In a 2001 study, scientists William T Harbaugh, Kate Krause, and Lise Vesterlund wanted to find out if children also gave their own possessions a higher value than those that belong to other people. And they do.

At the beginning of this experiment, 125 children are randomly divided into two groups: Group A and Group B. Group A are given a toy (for example, a bouncy ball) while Group B are given a different toy of equivalent value (say, an alien toy attached to a key ring). The children from Group A are then given the choice to trade their ball for the key-ring toy given to Group B, and vice versa. The scientists repeated this pattern four times, with similar low-value items. The results of their experiment are fascinating, because the majority of children succumbed to the endowment effect – simply, they rarely wanted to trade. Considering the toy they were first given to be 'better' or 'more valuable', children in both groups were 2.9 times more likely in both to stick with the first toy they were given, regardless of what the toy was. Basically, when we own something, we put a higher value on it than when we have to buy that object ourselves. Economists are fascinated by the endowment effect because it also happens to affect people who trade in hugely valuable items, like stocks and shares (and their actions can bring down whole economies). You've probably even noticed the endowment effect yourself, if you've ever tried to barter at a flea market or antiques store. People always think their junk is worth

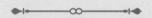

'It was found that people who placed a bet on a horse gave it a better chance of winning after they'd placed their bet than before'

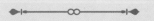

a lot more than you want to pay for it.

What this means for the magician is an increased audience fascination with any trick in which their own possessions are used. And that means bigger and better reactions should you have a camera team lurking close by. What's also interesting is that the Endowment Effect also seems to work on those members of the audience whose possessions are not being used, and this could simply be down to empathy. Our ability to put ourselves in the shoes of the man or woman called up on stage or stopped by the magician at a street corner means that we start to feel an empathetic version of the endowment effect ourselves. Watch Michael Carbonaro on YouTube and pay attention to how much you feel when you watch that guy get his car windows smashed; you're imagining you're him. Then there's the relief that it happened to him, and not you. Shock, horror, relief, and empathy are all bundled up in restoration magic.

LOOKING HARDER IN THE WRONG PLACES

The other – potentially powerful – result of the endowment effect is how it naturally makes an audience concentrate harder. So if I take a £20 note from you, we know you're going to care about it when it's ripped up into tiny pieces before your eyes. And we also know that you're going to care more than you would if I ripped up a piece of paper I took from my pocket. But this also means that when I use my skill as a magician to misdirect you (and I most certainly will), you'll simply be looking harder in the wrong place. This increased 'attentive blindness' is key to the likelihood of my trick succeeding. So let's take a closer look at attentive blindness, to see how it works.

THE INVISIBLE GORILLA

Attentive blindness means a failure to see what's right in front of you, and it was most famously demonstrated in the 1999 Invisible Gorilla test. Devised by psychologists Christopher Chabris and Daniel J Simons (whose fantastic book, *The Invisible Gorilla: And Other Ways Our Intuitions Deceive Us*, you may want to read), the Invisible Gorilla test is a brilliant experiment in which viewers are asked to watch two teams of people pass a ball to each other. One team has white T-shirts on, the other black. But you have to follow the white team and count how many passes they make. The entire test lasts less than a minute and a half and you can take it yourself on YouTube. What's fascinating is not how many passes the team makes (or how often people get that number right). It's the fact that a man in a gorilla suit enters the frame halfway through, beats his chest and then leaves. A gorilla! Right in front of you! But 50 per cent of people fail to see it.

This demonstrates that when we are asked to look at one specific thing, we concentrate on it so fully that we can often miss other – very dramatic – things. And this is central to a great deal of magic. Go back to that £20 note, which you earned, maybe in a job that you don't really love. It's your money, so it's worth more than the £20 notes of the jerk standing next to you. I've also just put it closer to you, in your personal space, so you can't help but focus your eyes on it. As a magician (and watch out for magicians when they do this), I may also be kinda bossy, and even tell you what to look at. 'Look at this,' is all I really have to say – and you'll obey, not only because the £20 is yours, but because under pressure, and in the spotlight, humans are submissive creatures – we do as we're told. You're becoming emotional (and we know this affects your judgement), you're confused, and I'm putting you under stress by tearing up the money. Is it any wonder that you miss the trick?

Above You care more if the banknote the magician is tearing in half in front of your eyes came from your own wallet.

Opposite When we are asked to concentrate fully on something, we often miss other – very dramatic – things.

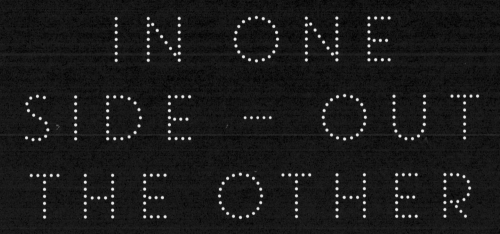

IN ONE SIDE – OUT THE OTHER

WHY PENETRATION TRICKS WORK

MATTER THROUGH MATTER

Penetration illusions are very simple; they're about making objects pass through other objects. Making a wine glass go through a table, making a large coin pass through the neck of a bottle, that sort of thing. But I have a theory about why these illusions are so effective: I think it's because we're reminded of their impossibility every day. Say you're slicing a tomato and your knife hits the cutting board or you're walking down the street looking at your phone and you bump into someone – these are both prompts. As we make our way through the world, we are constantly reminded of its basic physics; that there are rules about what can pass through what. In fact, these constant reminders are part of how we learn to navigate our way through life – just look at the toddler drunkenly swaying from sofa to chair leg or banging things against a table. By adulthood, we've learned instinctively what works and what doesn't and we know we can't walk though walls. We don't need to try it to find that out.

Any penetration illusion is therefore immediately going to be mind-blowing, because you're doing something that's usually reserved for metaphor. People say, 'I felt like I could walk through a brick wall,' and we take this to mean that they felt strong, invincible. So if you can really, literally, do it and walk through that wall, you have to contend with two things. The first one is shock (the 'What the…?!' reaction). And the second one is proving that you really did it.

Obviously you need to show the audience the item that's been penetrated both before and after the trick (so they can see it's intact). It's only magical to the audience if the object isn't damaged or tampered with and they have to know that these objects are solid and real. What you're doing here is letting the audience use the same senses that told them the trick was impossible to prove to them that it actually happened. It's also

'It's going to be mind-blowing, because you're doing something that's usually reserved for metaphor'

more impressive when you use everyday objects that audiences are familiar with; objects they instinctively understand the properties of. So, everyone knows that a brick wall is solid or that a glass bottle is solid. And that's why props are best when they're not things you'd only come across in magic shops. That's crucial to a lot of magic, because as soon the audience sees something that looks like a prop, alarm bells go off. People wonder why you've got a special chair or a special box and naturally wonder what purpose it could serve (other than facilitating the trick you're about to do).

THE IMPOSSIBLE, CLOSE UP

In a close-up situation, there are many different penetration illusions that look amazing. They also often sound fantastic, and we'll get to why that's important later. When you first see someone push a pen through a $1 bill that's come from your wallet, and when you get to inspect the note and can't find any rips, tears, or holes, it's a simple and beautiful thing. It works because it's your $1 bill (which goes back to the emotional investment we have in our own possessions, in the Restoration chapter, see pages 120–141). And it works because you

Above Everyone knows brick walls are solid. Or are they?

can get so close to the trick and inspect it; part of the beauty of a close-up penetration illusion is that you're so near to the magic.

Fay Presto is a brilliant close-up magician (she won The Magic Circle's Close-up Magician of the Year award in 2012), who does an incredible Bottle Through Table trick (you can see it on YouTube, if you search under her name). It's great because there's so much seamless and casual theatre involved – lots of taps to the table to prove the bottle and table are solid, real, and heavy; lots of natural, seemingly effortless patter (brilliant for distraction) and she involves the audience, asking them to help her push the bottle slowly through the table. It's really a masterclass in this kind of illusion.

There's also a fantastic Canadian magician called David Ben, who does a version of a trick called The Thumb Tie. It has a stately kind of pace to it, even though what he's doing feels potentially violent. I remember seeing him do this trick on a talk show. He's telling the host about a trip to Japan, where he was learning about ancient magic techniques, and on the desk between the two men are a beautiful, imposing Japanese sword, some ropes, and some protective gloves. David Ben tells the guy how he traded secrets with a Japanese master magician, who taught him how to bind his thumbs together with traditional Japanese paper cords (they look wiry and tough, like really thick pipe cleaners). He gets the host to tie first one, then another around both of his thumbs, wrapping and knotting them until his thumbs start to turn blue. 'Tighter, tighter,' he keeps saying, 'you must use a great deal of force here.' It's obviously making the host uncomfortable to tie these things, because he says 'Really? Tighter?' like he's scared he'll hurt him.

Once Ben's thumbs are bound together, he asks his host to put on the protective gloves and pick up the sword. This is when you see just how sharp that blade is. But the atmosphere Ben projects is still quite matter of fact – unshowy – and it's the host who doesn't look calm when he's asked to hold the sword up vertically, holding the tip with one hand and the handle with the other. He's told not to move and the camera comes in close now: we can see Ben press his hands together, so that his fingertips are just touching the edge of the blade, as if he's about to push the blade through the

Opposite Fay Presto is a genius of close-up magic – her Bottle Through Table trick will make you believe that a solid object can easily pass through a piece of wood.

space between his fingers and palms (but really he can't, because it looks as if it would take the skin off). Then he does a few practice 'pushes' as if he's making sure he's got his position right. And then all of a sudden Ben pushes his hands forwards towards the blade making this odd, breathy noise. Before you even have a chance to think about it, his hands have gone past the blade and are inside the loop created by the host's arms. And then – just as fast and just as calm – they're back again. What's fantastic is that you have this instrument capable of the most extreme violence and you're watching someone push their own flesh right through it. Like it's nothing, like it was butter.

BRICK WALLS, STEEL GATES & METAL PLATES

When you're performing penetration illusions on stage, rather than in close-up, you obviously have to think about scaling up in quite a big way. This makes it much more difficult to use objects that the audience believe are 'credible'. Whatever you use also has to work for someone sitting way back in a huge theatre, but at the same time the last thing you want is for everything on stage to look like a magician's gadget. This is even more crucial to modern audiences than it might once have been, because obviously at the turn of the 20th century – when magicians nearly always had crazy, weird, ornately painted boxes – no one really questioned it. In fact, I suspect the weirdness of magicians' props in those days was all part of that exotic ideal. The secret stuff they brought along to show you was precisely why you bought a ticket in the first place; you couldn't see these odd objects any other way. Now audiences are more knowledgeable, so you have to make everything less suspect and more organic – kind of, 'Hey, this is just normal stuff you have at home, therefore I can do magic.' Also, if you have credible props then it's more likely that the audience will attribute the magic to you, the performer, as opposed to the props. On stage – yet again – you also have to keep things simple. The more props there are, the more likely the audience will question what they're seeing.

Above Many magicians working at the turn of the 20th century used ornately painted boxes as props on stage.

Opposite David Ben, another Canadian illusionist, does a fantastic version of a trick called The Thumb Tie.

WALKING THROUGH WALLS

It was over a hundred years ago that Houdini first performed his Walking Through A Brick Wall illusion and many magicians have followed in his footsteps since – David Copperfield did it at The Great Wall of China. The reasons why it appeals to magicians are probably a little prosaic from the audience's point of view, in that it ticks boxes that are really only important for people in magic (that is, the fact that it's simple and it uses materials the audience are familiar with). Yet again, it's also an illusion that relies heavily on speed.

When Houdini first performed the illusion there was already a huge controversy about who had created the trick. Paying your dues is an important concept in magic, so when you base any illusion on someone else's idea, you're strongly advised to credit them. Houdini had bought the secret of the trick from a magician who may or may not have been the originator – so he may have thought he was in the clear – but the controversy might explain why he only performed the trick for a few weeks before passing it along to his brother, Hardeen. Either way, it's still a classic.

Houdini's wall was 9 feet by 10 feet, and there were screens on both sides that could conceal him. But he let the audience take a really good look at the wall, even letting a union of bricklayers inspect it with hammers for one performance (they also challenged Houdini to walk through a wall they had made – which, ever the showman, he did). He also let his spectators surround the wall on all sides during the performance, which is smart because it makes the illusion feel like close-up magic, even though it's on stage. (This is also smart from a naysayer's point of view, because if you get enough people up on stage you can eliminate the idea that the inspectors from the audience are stooges.) Then, to demonstrate just how quickly the penetration was achieved, Houdini would wave his hands above the screen on one side of the wall. His hands would quickly disappear, and then, just as fast, they'd reappear above the screen on the other side. It was quick. Crucially, it was just as quick as if he'd walked through that wall.

Opposite Siegfried & Roy performed a variation of the Interlude illusion, which involved a girl jumping through Roy's torso, followed by a tiger.

INTERLUDE

The Interlude illusion, first performed by husband-and-wife team The Pendragons, involves one performer appearing to push themselves straight through the body of another, from the back to the front. This trick is performed with the magician encased in a frame, his torso covered with a screen, thereby allowing the assistant to burst through or burn the screen away in a dramatic fashion. Siegfried & Roy later adapted the trick: in their version, the girl climbing through Roy's torso is followed by a tiger that appears to leap out from his chest.

WALKS THROUGH A BRICK WALL AND MYSTIFIES MAGICIANS

Houdini, the Handcuff King, Has a New Trick All to Himself—It Is Simple and Will Stand Close Watching, but Just How the "Elusive American" Gets on the Other Side Without Going Around or Over or Under Is Something That Neither Magic-Sleuths Nor Country Constables Nor the Bricklayers' Union Can Explain.

WATCH closely now, you clever ones. Here is a trick in magic which it will need all your cleverness to detect. It was recently shown in New York and is about the trickiest trick that has ever tricked a New York audience.

Not much paraphernalia here—just a big, brick wall built across the stage from back to front so that the audience can see both sides. A man is going to "walk through the wall" without displacing a single brick. Look sharp!

Can you examine the wall? Certainly you can. You can also examine the floor. You needn't stay out there in the auditorium. Go up on the stage. Form a half-circle of clever ones behind the wall and on both sides while the audience strains its eyes in front.

You can't find any trapdoors. If there were any they wouldn't do any good; the floor is covered with two large cloths, each a single piece. A man can't very well go through them without leaving a hole.

If he gets to the other side of the wall he won't do it by going down. Neither will he go up. The wall is just nine feet high and everybody can see over the top. And there isn't much chance of his going around either end with the audience sitting in front and you standing at the back.

Enter Harry Houdini, the "Handcuff King." The "Elusive American," they call him abroad. He stands solemnly beside the wall like a prisoner awaiting execution.

A little screen is placed around him. It is only six feet high and takes up not more than a third of the wall space. Another screen of the same size is placed on the other side of the wall.

Houdini's hands wave above the screen. "Here I am!" he cries. "Now I'm gone!"

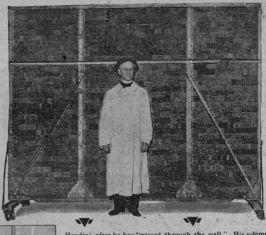

Houdini, after he has "passed through the wall." His solemn mien is like that of a prisoner awaiting execution.

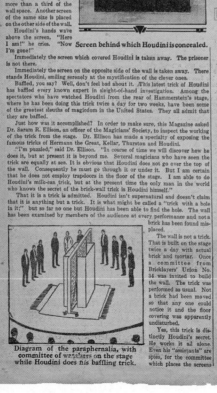

Screen behind which Houdini is concealed.

Immediately the screen which covered Houdini is taken away. The prisoner is not there.

Immediately the screen on the opposite side of the wall is taken away. There stands Houdini, smiling serenely at the mystification of the clever ones.

Baffled, you say? Well, don't feel bad about it. This latest trick of Houdini has baffled every known expert in sleight-of-hand investigation. Among the spectators who have watched Houdini from the rear of Hammerstein's stage, where he has been doing this trick twice a day for two weeks, have been some of the greatest sleuths of magicdom in the United States. They all admit that they are baffled.

Just how is it accomplished? In order to make sure, this Magazine asked Dr. Saram R. Ellison, an officer of the Magicians' Society, to inspect the working of the trick from the stage. Dr. Ellison has made a specialty of exposing the famous tricks of Hermann the Great, Kellar, Thurston and Houdini.

"I'm puzzled," said Dr. Ellison. "In course of time we will discover how he does it, but at present it is beyond me. Several magicians who have seen the trick are equally at sea. It is obvious that Houdini does not go over the top of the wall. Consequently he must go through it or under it. But I am certain that he does not employ trapdoors in the floor of the stage. I am able to do Houdini's milk-can trick, but at the present time the only man in the world who knows the secret of the brick-wall trick is Houdini himself."

That it is a trick is admitted. Houdini isn't supernatural and doesn't claim that it is anything but a trick. It is what might be called a "trick with a hole in it;" but so far no one but Houdini has been able to find the hole. The wall has been examined by members of the audience at every performance and not a brick has been found misplaced.

The wall is not a trick. That is built on the stage twice a day with actual brick and mortar. Once a committee from Bricklayers' Union No. 34 was invited to build the wall. The trick was performed as usual. Not a brick had been moved so that any one could notice it and the floor covering was apparently undisturbed.

Yes, this trick is distinctly Houdini's secret. He works it all alone. Even his "assistants" are spies, for the committee which places the screens

against the wall and takes them away again is selected from the audience.

Houdini isn't saying that the trick will never be detected. He isn't saying anything. He is just doing the trick and letting the public guess. He wants to be watched. Being watched has been his chief enjoyment from the time he first bewildered country constables by slipping out of their handcuffs more quickly than they could slip them on. There is only one thing which he possibly enjoys more, and that is watching the faces of his audience when he has accomplished his trick.

And he finds but little difference in the facial expressions, whether the onlookers be country constables or blase denizens of Broadway. On this, as on other occasions, they prove themselves brothers "under their skins." And when they show their amazement at discovering Houdini on the side of the wall where they all knew he was going to be there is one face in the theatre which seems to show more real enjoyment than any other. That is Houdini's.

Diagram of the paraphernalia, with committee of watchers on the stage while Houdini does his baffling trick.

MY BRICK WALL

Penn & Teller say they have three rules of magic…

1. Never do the same trick twice
2. Never reveal how it's done
3. Never let the audience see your preparation

It's number 2 I'm interested in here. Because, although most people believe that no one in magic ever reveals how their tricks are done, the fact is that magicians reveal their secrets all the time – at lectures you could easily go to, at conventions the public can pay to attend, and in DVDs you can buy. They do this to share knowledge and to sell their ideas to other magicians all over the world who want to perform the same tricks. The people who really 'give things away' fall into another category – YouTube account holders with an axe to grind, people who just really, really, really hate magicians. Obviously this kind of stuff upsets us because, if you're giving away secrets to our potential audience, it ruins all the fun as well as shrinking the market. I think this is particularly true when you see a magician's performance reduced to a few slow-mo gifs. That's kind of sad. All that said, I do understand the fascination with uncovering the methods of magic. I've met people who say they hate magic because they can't stand the not knowing – it drives them crazy that they can't work out how tricks are done. Most people will try to work it out, but then eventually just settle for feeling good about the fact that a brilliant illusion isn't easy to work out; it should make the magic more, not less, satisfying.

So you can understand why there have been people who wanted to reveal Houdini's secrets ever since he first performed. That's certainly true of the Brick Wall illusion – there was even a documentary that revealed how it was done. That meant I had to be really careful when I started thinking about performing it. The people I work with and I knew the secret had been revealed, so we had to perform it in such a way that the 'Houdini method' was eliminated. We had to tackle that revealed secret head-on, so that

'I've met people who say they hate magic because they can't stand the not knowing'

Opposite Houdini's Brick Wall illusion fascinated audiences – there was even a documentary revealing how it was done.

Overleaf This is one of the penetration illusions I perform in my show.

'In a challenge piece like this you want to spell out where you're coming from'

even if you knew how Houdini did it, you would understand I wasn't doing it the same way.

This had a huge effect on both the presentation and the planning. From a presentation point of view, it's not an incredibly visual illusion because obviously I'm hidden behind the screens. This makes it more of a puzzle, and the audience's job is to work out how it happened after they've been given the chance to examine everything. Then, from a planning point of view, we had to find a way for you to see that I couldn't just go under the wall like Houdini might have. We did this by adding in a metal plate, made of steel, and putting that under the wall. We slowly eliminated every possible way it could have been done.

I tackle these objections head on in my narration. In a challenge piece like this you want to spell out where you're coming from and it's also a good opportunity to pay homage to Houdini (when I performed it in Blackpool for my ITV special, it was exactly a hundred years since the illusion had been done in the UK). I tell the audience how my brick wall is 8 feet tall and 9 feet wide and made up of '2 tonnes of solid mass'. This wall is 2,200 pounds of steel beams filled in with 2,200 pounds of bricks, plus it's been constructed by bricklayers (it's BIG). Then I invite the bricklayers on stage, because I want the audience to get to know them well enough to know they're not stooges and because it's useful for the audience to know how they built it – how each course of bricks was laid, how the final steel was bolted on top. The audience even gets to see a sped-up film of the wall taking shape. If you're lucky, the bricklayers will say something perfect like mine did in Blackpool: 'It's basically like any wall in any

house in Britain. You can move it with a mechanical digger, but other than that, it's not going anywhere.' Which, of course, is exactly what you want your bricklayers to say.

I then bring down my steel plate from the rafters of the theatre, while five people are picked randomly from the audience to join the three bricklayers. Then I let the inspections begin – eight people tapping and banging the steel plate with hammers and checking it from either side and then doing the same with the wall. The steel plate is lowered to the stage floor and the wall is wheeled over it. I also decided to wear a chest-mounted GoPro, so you could see the performance from my point of view. Now, it's time to begin: 'I can't go around the wall because of the spectators, I can't go under the wall because of the steel plate, and I can't go over the wall because you'd see me.'

A screen is put in place on either side of the wall. They're openwork screens with roller blinds in the frame so the audience can see me standing by the wall until I pull the blinds down. The screens are also smaller and less wide than the metal plate (they take up about the floor space of a phone booth) so you can see that there's no way for me to sneak under the edge of the steel plate without being seen. The blinds come down…there's a moment… and then they're up again. I'm through. It doesn't make sense.

SEPARATING THE METHOD FROM THE EFFECT

Separating the method (how a trick is done) from the effect (the trick itself) is one of magic's golden rules. You'll remember this from the Production chapter (see pages 10–33)– you have to find a way to get your 'secret' as far away as possible from the actual 'meat' of the trick. A good example of this might be a disappearance illusion, because ideally I will have vanished the object long before you think. Then, by the time I tell you the disappearance is happening, it'll be impossible for you to see. In practical terms, this might mean

Opposite David Copperfield famously performed a penetration illusion where he appeared to walk through the Great Wall of China.

I hide the real disappearance (pocketing a coin, say) and act like the coin is still in my hand until I fake *another disappearance*: the one I want you to see. All this means is that the most 'heat' in a magic trick is when the trick happens for the magician and the audience at the same time. When you have to do the secret move right in front of them, that's when you need the most skill.

THE PROPS ARE REAL: MEANINGLESS NOISE

Another way to fool you into thinking that the trick (or effect) hasn't taken place yet is by using sound. Luckily this is quite easy with penetration illusions, because the magician will need to prove to you that the objects they're using are real. Obviously, nearly all the objects you're going to want to use for a penetration illusion are solid, because there's no trick in making a piece of putty penetrate a bottle. So there's a lot of bashing and tapping and knocking going on during a penetration illusion – large metal rings against each other, coins against glass, glass against table. All these sounds are telling your brain two things on a fairly basic level: one, that the object making the noise is still in the magician's hand and, two, that the object is solid (so it can't possibly pass through another object). Noise is much more powerful than if I told you that a coin or glass bottle was real. If I was vanishing a coin and I said 'Now, this is obviously a real coin,' I'd be putting doubt into your mind – doubt that might not have been there if I'd just tapped the coin against the table.

What the noise does, therefore, is to reinforce a belief that you already have. On a conscious or subconscious level, you know that coins are solid and that solid things make noises when you bash them together. What it also does – and this is the cleverest bit, because it's a brilliant piece of misdirection – is to tell you where that coin is in space and time. Your brain has no reason to doubt that the coin is in my hand, because you heard the tap when I brought my hand down onto the table. And this piece of aural information (which you've used to make your conclusion that the coin is in my hand) falls in line with every other time you heard

Opposite Toppling dominoes are a good example of cause and effect. Causal inference happens when cause and effect get mixed up.

a solid object make a noise. If you think about it, you hear solid objects make sounds hundreds if not thousands of times a day – when you're washing dishes, putting down your laptop, moving a chair. However, if you believe the coin is still in my hand just because you heard the noise (and not because you saw it there), we're dealing with something called 'causal inference'.

'Your brain has no reason to doubt that the coin is in my hand, because you heard the tap when I brought my hand down onto the table'

CAUSAL INFERENCE

Let's break it down. It's called causal inference because this phenomenon is about humans mixing up cause and effect. You hear a noise, and you *infer* that you know what *caused* it. This reinforcement happens partly because you have established beliefs, but it also shows that people often don't need solid proof to believe in something. This is often true in situations where people use pseudo-science to explain how they became healthier ('I ate kale and now I no longer have cancer' does not mean that kale cures cancer, for example). If we're smart, we will take the totality of someone's health into account – plus the evidence of a good number of other scientifically studied people – before we believe any claims about miracle cures or miraculous effects. Another good example would be from the world of entertainment, where you'll often hear musicians or actors talk about pieces of clothing

or objects they've imbued with a talismanic quality. If an actor wore red socks when giving the performance for which they were awarded an Oscar, they may come to view those socks as lucky. But just because two pieces of information are linked doesn't mean that one causes the other.

In magic, of course, we have come to love and rely on human assumptions. In fact, we actively seek out situations where we can force you to come to false conclusions (especially, as I say, if those conclusions are about time or the sequence of events in a trick). We know that when the audience is watching magic, they aren't looking for a timeline. We also know they won't know that a trick has begun until we show them that it has – either verbally, via movement, or by using sound. It's only when the audience has picked up on those cues, and when they believe the trick has 'started' that they really start paying attention and looking for your secrets. Hopefully, by that point, they've already missed them.

Opposite Sportsmen, musicians, and actors often have talismans, like this sailor's lucky red socks.

ESCAPING THE JAWS OF DEATH

ESCAPOLOGY AS AN ART FORM

WHAT IS ESCAPOLOGY?

Escapology differs from other forms of magic because it casts the magician as the hero of the piece. In other illusions, you could argue that the focus is largely on the magician (me) trying to fool the audience (you) – so the power balance is a little off, and I have knowledge that you don't. In escapology, however, we're essentially on the same side. You're watching me overcome a terrifying physical challenge and you (hopefully!) want me to succeed. The power I do have, of course, is in knowing how much danger there really is.

Of course, the main hurdle when performing an escape is scepticism, because escapology is the kind of magic where it's logical to assume there's a trick involved. The audience is bound to be thinking, 'Why would you put yourself in that kind of peril, night after night?' My first job, therefore, is to make sure that the threat is authentic, so the audience can feel the pressure I'm under. My second job is to have trained and practised enough that I can escape that threat every time. More than any other form of stage magic, escapes have to be planned meticulously. The skilled magician will think about presentation, pacing, jeopardy, and fear if they really want to make the audience gasp.

FEATS OF ENDURANCE

If you could provoke just one feeling in your audience when performing an escape, it would be awe. Think about those rare moments when you feel a sense of wonder about what human beings are capable of and most people will mention inspiring events like the Olympics. And if you've ever lived in a city that has hosted the Olympics, you'll recognize this feeling and how uplifting it is – how you can get swept away by seeing feats of athletic endeavour and how these superhumans who train so hard give us hope. I have to tap into that feeling, so that the relief is

Opposite Houdini performed his Upside Down Straitjacket Escape in a number of cities, including London.

audible when I finally escape. I also need to convince you that I'm strong enough to fight my way out of a straitjacket, even if I'm upside down. What's satisfying for me here is that escapology is a demonstrable skill. If curtains or sheets aren't hiding me from view, then I get to show you I can really do it. This is unlike pretty much every other form of magic, where I have to do the opposite and hide my skill. In sleight of hand, the audience only gets to see the result of your skill, not the sleights themselves.

What we're doing here is not unlike the plot of most action movies – the audience knows in its heart that the hero is going to succeed and live to see the final reel, but it also knows that most human beings couldn't drive a car from one Abu Dhabi skyscraper to another without killing themselves. You suspend your disbelief for the *Fast & Furious* franchise just like you do when you watch me escape from the Jaws of Death. Just because it's ridiculous, doesn't mean it's not fun.

COMEDY VS. DANGER

Close-up escapes differ from their stage counterparts in that the magician is usually in a lot less danger, so some close-up escapology illusions are played for laughs. One of the most famous is called the Rope Tie, which the magician performs sitting down on a chair. A helper (usually picked from the audience), watches as you take a piece of strong rope and wind it around and underneath your knees until you've tied your legs together. Then you tie your wrists to your legs and ask the helper to cover your hands and knees with their jacket. The comic aspect is that most magicians can get out of this restraint in a heartbeat, so, as soon as the jacket is covering their legs, they'll pull one hand out from under

Above Houdini in his straitjacket.

168

it, point to the helper and say, 'No, no, stand further over there,' and then put their hand back, carrying on with the trick. This makes the helper do double-takes because they often don't clock that the magician keeps 'escaping' – or, at least, they catch on slower than the audience.

The first time you see the Rope Tie, it's fun. But for me, it's got nothing on stage escapes or large-scale performances because obviously at no point does it seem dangerous. I absolutely love escapology, so I get uncomfortable when it's reduced to something cheesy, and I'm not crazy about illusions where the magician is doing the same, off-the-peg patter as anyone else who's bought that routine. If you see someone do any trick too many times it's like hearing the same joke over and over again. I also think it's kind of douchey if your routine uses an audience member as a whipping boy – making jokes at the audience's expense is kind of lame. For me, it can tip over into arrogance and you look like you're saying, 'Look at how great I am,' which is exactly what I try to avoid in my own performance. I feel like you're undermining both the audience and the magic itself when that happens.

'What's satisfying for me is that escapology is a demonstrable skill. If curtains or sheets aren't hiding me from view, then I get to show you I can really do it.'

FAILURE MEANS A DROWNING DEATH!

It's not possible to write about escapology without mentioning Harry Houdini. For most magicians he's the ultimate showman – a performer who knew exactly how powerful great magic could be and who knew how to maximize publicity for everything he did. It's no accident that his escapes are considered to be the most iconic, or that he's the one person in magic most people could name. Anyone performing escapology illusions today owes him a huge debt of gratitude, not least me.

One of his most famous and ground-breaking escapes was the Chinese Water Torture Cell. In it, his feet would be would be fastened into stocks before he was hung upside down from a frame. This frame was lowered and became the lid of an overflowing tank of water, where Houdini would hang, submerged and shackled. Curtains would be hung around the tank so that Houdini could not be seen, adding to the drama and provoking anxiety levels in the audience to rise. An orchestra would play a sad popular song called *Asleep in the Deep* (sample lyric: 'Many brave hearts are asleep in the deep, So beware! beware!') and an assistant stood by with an axe, in case something went wrong. But each time Houdini would make a dramatic escape from the cell after a few minutes of agonized waiting. Naturally, the audiences went wild.

Houdini was a master at exploiting the fears of his audience. He knew perfectly well how common certain phobias are; that many of us have nightmares involving drowning or claustrophobia. He was also incredible at harnessing the media, making headlines in every city he performed in. Another of his illusions – the Upside Down Straitjacket Escape – would be performed opposite the buildings that housed each city's biggest newspapers. High up in the air, writhing in a straitjacket, he could guarantee a great write-up and

HOUDINI
PRESENTS HIS OWN ORIGINAL INVENTION
THE GREATEST SENSATIONAL MYSTERY
EVER ATTEMPTED IN THIS OR ANY OTHER AGE!!!

£200 REWARD TO ANY ONE PROVING THAT IT IS POSSIBLE TO OBTAIN AIR IN THE UP-SIDE-DOWN POSITION IN WHICH HOUDINI RELEASES HIMSELF FROM THIS WATER-FILLED-TORTURE-CELL.

Above and opposite Houdini's ground-breaking escape: the Chinese Water Torture Cell.

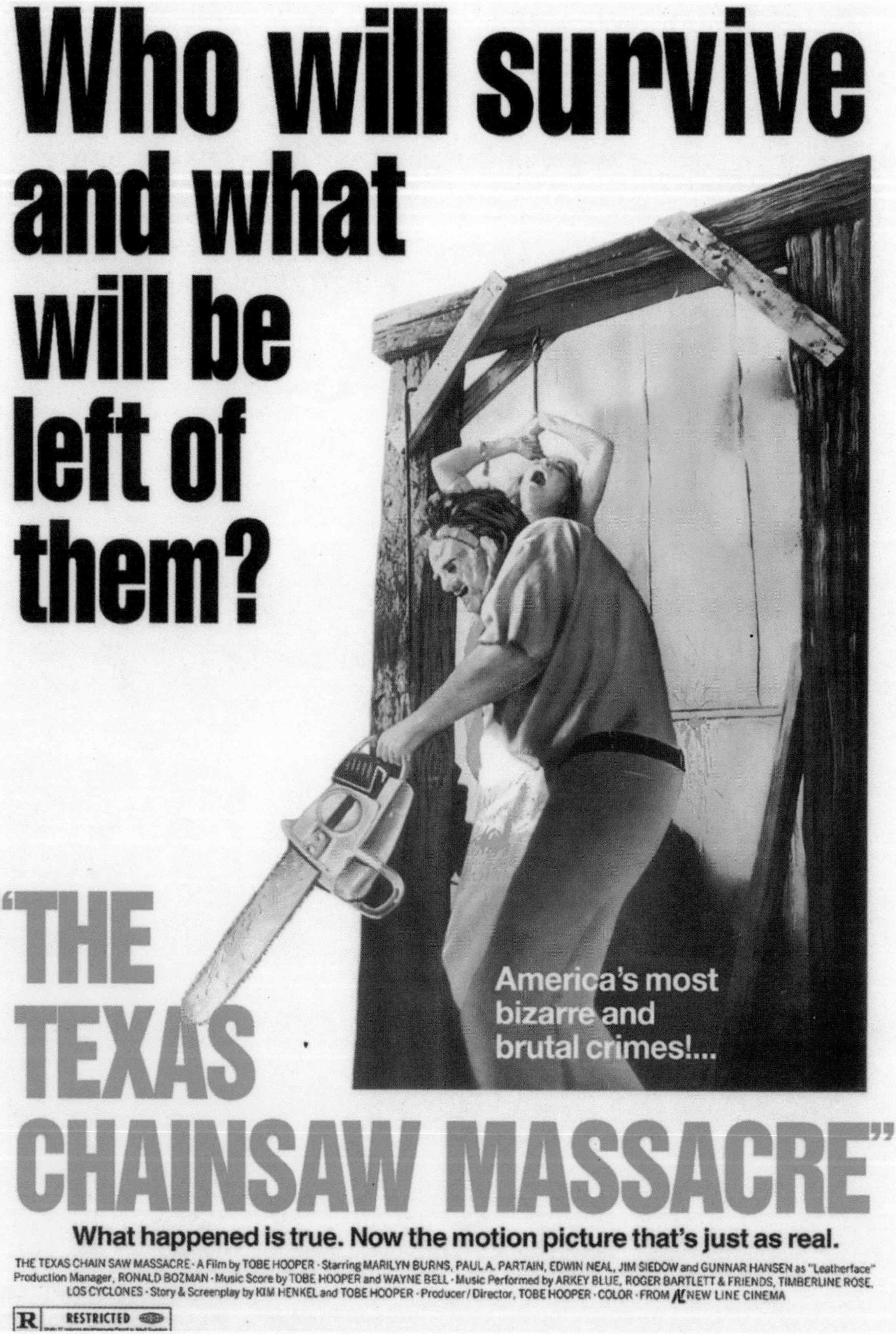

Who will survive and what will be left of them?
"THE TEXAS CHAINSAW MASSACRE"
America's most bizarre and brutal crimes!...
What happened is true. Now the motion picture that's just as real.
THE TEXAS CHAIN SAW MASSACRE · A Film by TOBE HOOPER · Starring MARILYN BURNS, PAUL A. PARTAIN, EDWIN NEAL, JIM SIEDOW and GUNNAR HANSEN as "Leatherface"
Production Manager, RONALD BOZMAN · Music Score by TOBE HOOPER and WAYNE BELL · Music Performed by ARKEY BLUE, ROGER BARTLETT & FRIENDS, TIMBERLINE ROSE, LOS CYCLONES · Story & Screenplay by KIM HENKEL and TOBE HOOPER · Producer/Director, TOBE HOOPER · COLOR · FROM NEW LINE CINEMA
R RESTRICTED

a sell-out show in every city. If he was around today, his work would definitely go viral.

Houdini's performances also give us the perfect template for how escape illusions should be done. First, he knew that he had to deal with the sceptics, so he spent a great deal of time at the beginning of his shows getting the audience to check all the equipment (locks, shackles, water tank, straitjacket) to reassure them nothing was dodgy. Next, there's his music and that creepy song about sailors drowning at sea. Then there's that axe. Yes, it's the quickest way to get him out if something goes wrong, but how could it be the safest? Imagine the glass smashing and what would happen to his body if it was propelled over the broken glass. That's a potentially terrible and violent image, and I can't help thinking it's what Houdini wanted us to think about, subconsciously or not. Even the curtains, though it seems counterintuitive, serve a purpose. One, they obviously stop us from seeing what's really going on, which is great for Houdini. And they also forced the audience to imagine what was happening. And sometimes, that's more powerful than actually seeing the action.

If you've ever sat through *The Texas Chainsaw Massacre*, you know what I'm on about. Stephen King – of all people – called the film a work of 'cataclysmic terror'. But when you actually see the movie, a great deal of that terror is supplied through your imagination – the lighting is often deliberately indistinct and a great deal of the violence is merely glimpsed; there aren't many lingering shots. The documentary filmmaker Jesse Stommel, in an essay he wrote for the film journal *Bright Lights*, wrote that, 'much of the horror of *The Texas Chainsaw Massacre* is something we unleash upon ourselves'. In magic and theatre as well as movies, these techniques have long been used for good reason. When the audience could hear Houdini sploshing around – but couldn't see what he was doing or if he was okay – their brains filled in the gaps in horrific ways, making them more afraid.

In Houdini's Milk Can Escape – where he was shackled and put into a water-filled milk can just large for him to fit into – he also

Opposite Stephen King called *The Texas Chainsaw Massacre* a work of 'cataclysmic terror', but much of the fear is down to your imagination, rather than what is happening on screen.

HOUDINI AND MISS UNDINA

One of the most notable feuds in the world of magic was that between Harry Houdini (1874–1926) and a woman known as Miss Undina. She had advertised her version of Houdini's Chinese Water Torture Cell act, an escape that involved the magician being locked in stocks, suspended upside down, and lowered into a glass tank filled with water, which was then also locked. Houdini sued her for copying his act and won, resulting in Miss Undina having to destroy all her promotional posters. Very few of the posters survived, but one of them was saved by Houdini himself – with the lesson being that you should never mess with Harry Houdini.

encouraged audiences to hold their breath along with him, to see how long they could last. I love this detail because you can almost hear it; the tense silence of the theatre, broken only by panicked gasps from the audience as slowly, one by one, they could hold their breath no longer.

THE JAWS OF DEATH

Without sounding like a sicko, your fear is part of the appeal of performing an escape. That's because I know that if I can make you feel anxious, you'll enjoy it more. Nowadays you have to up the ante, because people are conditioned to seeing crazy and ridiculous things all the time. Just hanging upside down and doing a straitjacket escape in this day and age isn't as effective as it once was. If I was just strapped to a frame, upside down and hanging by a rope, people would think 'Oh, okay.' But if the rope was on FIRE, and there was a nice, big shark tank below me, then it's like, 'Wooooah.' Within reason, you have to up the stakes.

I also wanted to avoid being the kind of escapologist who acts like they're superior – all cheesy hand gestures and big hair. This can be quite common in magic and I think it goes back to insecurity – magicians often get into magic in adolescence when they're unsure of themselves. They see magic as a way of learning to do something most people could never do. It also becomes a way to communicate with people (it certainly was for me). But then there's a fine line about how you use that knowledge. If you flaunt it or use escapology for laughs, it demeans the method and cheapens it. Being able to escape from restraints should feel like a powerful thing, not something throwaway or easily dismissed.

PLANNING MY ESCAPE

Everybody knows what it's like to be underwater. Fear of drowning is pretty universal. Falling, not being able to breathe, confined spaces, fire, sharp objects – we'd all rather avoid those, too. So I have to find a way to invoke these fears without making the illusion

'Your fear is part of the appeal of performing an escape. If I can make you feel anxious, you'll enjoy it more'

Opposite A poster for Miss Undina's water cell act, which landed her in a feud with Harry Houdini for copying his act.

too complicated. If it's all, 'This rope is connected to this, which is connected to this bag of sand, which will be released by this monkey, after this rope has burned through and that bell has rung,' it won't work. The mechanics of how the danger is going to reach you have to be as direct as possible. A ridiculously complicated-looking machine isn't inherently scary, and a simple mechanism also helps eliminate the opportunity for trickery. From your perspective as a viewer, the less there is for you to look at, the more fair and believable the whole thing becomes.

I work with a team of people I respect and admire when I plan my shows, and I guess I rely on them even more when we're designing escapology illusions because, by their very nature, they're more dangerous. So we focused on simplicity for the Jaws of Death, eventually ending up with a huge, steel bear trap that's suspended from the rafters of the theatre. I'm hanging upside down between the two enormous claws. I'm also in a straitjacket and I have to get out before a burning rope snaps the jaws shut. That sounds like a lot of elements but it's actually pretty simple: rope breaks = dead Darcy.

BIG SHINY MACHINES

We also had to make sure that the jaws looked as big and as menacing as possible. Sense of scale is important in most escapology illusions but there are exceptions. Obviously you don't want your Upside Down Water Torture Cell to look like a roomy swimming pool. But for the jaws it wouldn't look scary if there were two ball-peen hammers that were about to come down on either side of my face. It might hurt, but it wouldn't have been much to look at. So the bear claws are huge, shiny, and sharp. There are practical considerations, too. The illusion has to travel with you all over the world and still be relatively easy and safe to set up in each theatre. It's got to work seamlessly hundreds of times on stage, in front of thousands of people.

Opposite and overleaf I'm hanging upside down between two huge jaws, in a straitjacket. The rope keeping the jaws apart is set on fire, giving me little time to escape.

PRACTICE MAKES PERFECT

Once your contraption is set, you can get down to training. Obviously, to perform an escape you need to be physically fit. But the amount of training you need to do depends on the illusion itself. It can test the limits of human endurance – even something as common as an escape from a straitjacket is a physically difficult thing. You've got to stretch your shoulders so you can get your arms over your head, and that means a lot of time in the gym.

Let's go back to Houdini's Milk Can Escape. He was handcuffed and the can was full of water. It's pretty horrible when you think about it. It also had a great poster strapline that makes me think of horror movies ('Failure Means A Drowning Death!'). But whatever you think, and no matter how he really got out of the can, he still had to hold his breath for a very long time. And that's always going to be risky and dangerous. I've been talking about performing something like this for a while and the preparation for it comes in long before you actually build the illusion. You have to very slowly and carefully build up your ability to hold your breath, and you do this by getting a lot of expert advice and doing things like free diving or breathing exercises. Basically, you need to spend a lot of time increasing your lung capacity, day by day and week by week and month by month – until you stop panicking.

PSYCHOLOGY VS. PHYSIOGNOMY

This, actually, is the biggest hurdle you encounter in training. Most people, with a good trainer and enough time in the gym, can build up their physical stamina until they're fit enough to perform. But it's much harder to keep your brain on track. From a psychological point of view, you have to be able to keep calm and keep your heart rate down. Not panicking when you hold your breath is the hardest thing because, as your body is telling you it's time to panic, the stress hormone cortisol is flooding your system and your body, naturally, wants out. The dull truth is, the only way around this is to keep practising.

'Whatever you think, and no matter how he really got out of the can, he still had to hold his breath for a very long time'

Opposite Houdini's Milk Can Escape saw him handcuffed inside a large metal can filled with water.

What's also kind of weird about all the preparation is that it's the part of being an illusionist that contrasts most fully with being on stage. I know I need to spend hours on my own until I can hold my breath for minutes at a time without the stress responses in my body kicking in. I don't need a breathing consultant in my entourage to learn this stuff, it's just dedication. You also have to have endure a lot of something not working before you perfect it and can show it to an audience. When it doesn't work, it's dangerous. The good thing is that I don't feel fear very easily, and in a sick sort of way I really like being in danger and getting myself out of those situations. I'm not going to lie; the adrenaline pop feels good.

BATMAN

For the Jaws of Death, you also have to get used to being upside down. Moving around there, getting used to it, so you can tell what it's going to feel like at every second of the performance. I did have to go a little vampiric for a month or two, tying my feet to a bar and just hanging there until I could turn off the part of my brain that panics when the blood has rushed to my head. That's the biggest part of that challenge physically, because you can go blind or blackout if you're not in control or if you've not trained hard enough. You need to have a lot of strength in your core, too, so I'll incorporate lots of planks and stomach crunches into my gym routine, and then test out my stomach muscles while I'm hanging there.

You also have to prepare in stages. So I'll get used to hanging upside down, and then separately get used to escaping from a straitjacket, before I put both things together and escape upside down. I mean, there were moments in rehearsal where I was like, 'Holy crap, this is messed up,' and, when I first saw the bear claws, that's what I thought because I still couldn't believe they will sell these things to people. Overall, it was something like three or four months of pure physical training before we even attempted a proper rehearsal. The whole process of preparing for an escape can take up to a year, if not more.

FEAR & ESCAPOLOGY

As I've mentioned, in order for the escape to have power, I need you to be scared and to remind you of things you're already afraid of on a pretty basic human level. This makes it more enjoyable for you in the end, because you'll feel greater relief the more you think I'm in danger. From a psychological point of view, however, it's also worth bearing in mind that when you feel fear, your ability to process information is different. And that can be useful to me as a magician.

It's also true to say that the more primal fears I can play on, the better. I don't want to sound mean here, but I try to play on as many as possible. And it's easy enough for a magician or illusionist to find out what these are – we have anthropologists and psychologists who've done all the work for us. If you look up those research papers, you'll also see that what mankind is afraid of has changed over the years, so that what people reported being scared of in 1968 is different to what they're afraid of now. Age matters too, because children are frightened of different things than adults, and adults are scared of different things than seniors. Men and women are also often afraid of different stuff. So a really good magician will make sure he knows exactly what the general public are most afraid of at that point in time. And a *really smart magician* will have a team of brilliant magic consultants to do that research for him.

The great thing is that, even if you're not afraid of drowning, but have more of a problem with something like confined spaces or, say, snakes, it won't really matter. Nearly all of our fears can be reduced to one basic, vital thing: not being in control. Danger that

Above Nearly all of our fears can be reduced to one basic, vital thing: not being in control.

is unpredictable – whatever form it comes in – is the most potent and frightening thing of all. When you can perceive danger, but you don't know when it's going to strike, your brain can't help but panic. And that's why the ticking clock plays such an important part in escapology.

TIME BOMBS

Any illusion where you can introduce time, or more specifically a deadline, gets people worried. This is one of the things I like most about the Jaws of Death, because the rope holding the jaws apart is burning and the audience doesn't really know when it'll snap. What this is doing to you as a viewer is to put you under extreme pressure, which in turn changes the way your brain processes what you see.

A good example of this, and one that most people can relate to, happens at school. Think of the last time you had to do any kind of exam under timed conditions. Nearly everyone has been in that situation, surrounded by other people taking the same test, so quiet you can hear a pin drop. But what happens? Suddenly your ability to read becomes impaired, and you find yourself reading the question over and over again. It takes skill, and practice, to calm yourself down, and not everybody can – some will miss a whole, vital part of the exam question and fail as a result. The point about escapology is that the audience doesn't really have time to prepare the brain or get it ready for this pressure, so it's even more likely that everyone will be in a state of mild panic. You'll be looking at the person next to you, looking all over the stage, you just won't see things as clearly. Basically, audiences go crazy for a ticking clock.

LIKEABILITY VS. HATE-WATCHING

Escapology is also much more powerful if you're actually invested in the person who's escaping. So, in order for you to get the most out of it, you need to want me to survive. You could argue that it goes both ways (if they really hate you, maybe they'll be just as interested in the outcome?), but I'd certainly hope that most people who come to see me don't think I'm a jerk. One way around this, for me, was to include personal elements in the Jaws of Death illusion, things that tell you about who I am and where I came from. Because people have seen straitjacket escapes before, you have to find new ways to connect with the audience. Including family photos and home movies in the Jaws of Death was one way to do this.

This also helps if you're trying to convince the audience that you're not just some cheesy guy on stage. The video of me that plays during Jaws of Death has old family home movies and photos that show me as an innocent, smiling little boy, before I was famous. The fact that my life is literally flashing before my eyes adds a whole other layer to the illusion (as well as sneakily giving you even more things to look at and for your brain to process). It should make it clear that I'm a real person, who's prepared to put his life on the line for your entertainment.

Above The video that plays while I perform Jaws of Death includes photos of me as a boy, long before I was famous.

Opposite The Capilano Canyon Suspension Bridge was used by scientists to test for the correlation between fear and attraction.

WE WANT TO BE SCARED: FEAR & SEX

If you've ever wondered why we like to be scared (rollercoasters, horror movies, ghost trains) then the obvious answer is that we get a kick out of the adrenaline rush. But what a lot of people don't

know is that fear also makes human beings feel sexy. There have been a few studies that have tried to work out how closely the two feelings – fear and sexual arousal – are linked, and it's worth thinking about that from the magician's point of view. Without wanting to sound cynical and jaded, anything that makes you come back to see my show again has got to be pretty good, right? And yet again, feeling sexy gives your brain more things to process, which means it's harder for you to spot how I do it.

One study in particular demonstrates this link quite well, I think. In 1974, scientists Donald G Dutton and Arthur P Aron wanted to investigate what scientific evidence there could be for 'heightened sexual arousal under conditions of high anxiety'. Their first experiment was 'designed to test the notion that an attractive female is seen as more attractive by males who encounter her while they experience a strong emotion (fear) than by males not experiencing a strong emotion'. They did this by choosing two very different bridges that (male, straight) participants had to cross, and by then asking the men to interact with an attractive woman. This is from the research paper:

'The "experimental" bridge was the Capilano Canyon Suspension Bridge, a 5-foot-wide, 450-foot-long, bridge constructed of wooden boards attached to wire cables that ran from one side to the other of the Capilano Canyon. The bridge has many arousal-inducing features such as (a) a tendency to tilt, sway, and wobble, creating the impression that one is about to fall over the side; (b) very low handrails of wire cable which contribute to this impression; and (c) a 230-foot drop to rocks and shallow rapids below the bridge. The "control" bridge was a solid wood bridge further upriver. Constructed of heavy cedar, this bridge was wider and firmer than the experimental bridge, was only 10 feet above a small, shallow rivulet which ran into the main river, had high handrails, and did not tilt or sway.

'As subjects crossed either the control or experimental bridge, they were approached by the Female interviewer. The interviewer explained that she was doing a project for her psychology class on the effects of exposure to scenic attractions on creative expression. She then asked potential subjects if they would fill out a short questionnaire...On the second page, subjects were instructed to write a brief, dramatic story based upon a picture of a young woman covering her face with one hand and reaching with the other.

'On completion of the questionnaire, the interviewer thanked the subject and offered to explain the experiment in more detail when she had more time. At this point, the interviewer tore the corner off a sheet of paper, wrote down her name and phone number, and invited each subject to call, if he wanted to talk further.'

What the scientists did, was
1. Analyse the stories written by the men for 'sexual imagery',
2. Count how many of the men took the attractive woman's phone number and
3. Count how many men phoned the woman to 'discuss the study'.

'It was designed to test the notion that an attractive female is seen as more attractive by males who encounter her while they experience a strong emotion (fear)'

The scientists discovered that the men who crossed the scary bridge wrote stories which had 1.75 times (or 75 per cent) more sexual imagery. The men who crossed the sexy bridge were also four times more likely to call the woman. Basically, they were more attracted to her when they'd just experienced 'high anxiety'.

Obviously, experiments like this aren't concrete proof. In this study, the sample size was quite small and it's hard to measure what counts as an objectively 'attractive woman' when we all have different tastes and predilections. But similar experiments have been conducted (one asked participants to rate the attractiveness of people in photos before and after going on a rollercoaster and – yes, you've guessed it – they gave higher scores after the ride) which make the same connection. I also think that if you've ever snuggled up to someone when watching a horror film, you'll understand. 'High anxiety' explains pretty well how I feel when I'm doing the Jaws of Death. And if I perform it well, you're going to feel it, too.

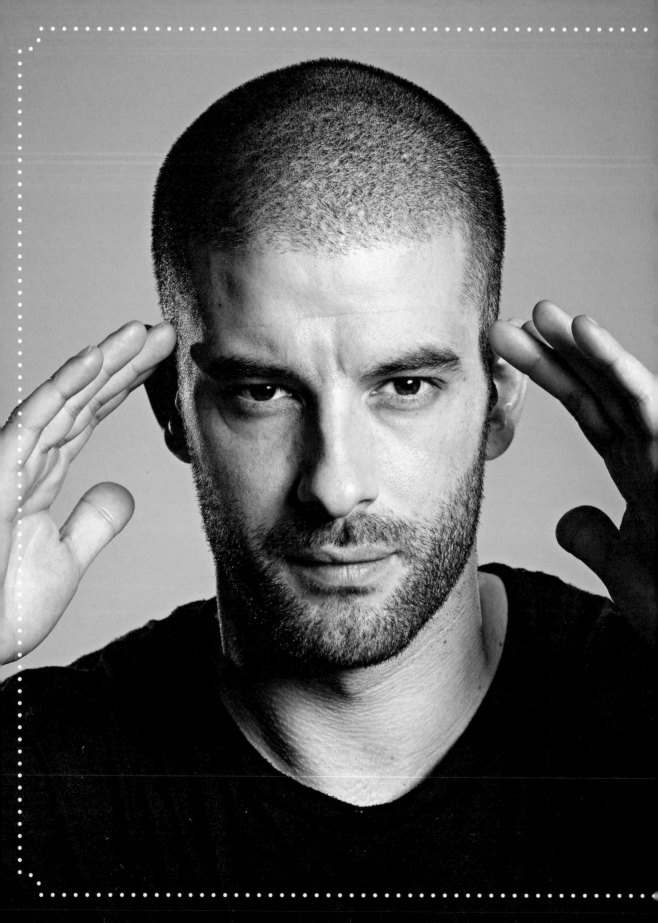

LOOK INTO
MY EYES

THE ART OF MIND READING
& PREDICTION

WHAT IS MENTALISM?

Mentalism and mind reading belong to a very distinct category of illusion that tends to stand apart from the rest of magic craft. It's a rich and historic form of magic that uses clever and sophisticated psychological techniques, some of which I'll explain here, to fool you. What you tend to find, though, is that most mentalists will specialize in mental illusions (predicting the outcome of things, being able to read people's minds, seemingly having extra-sensory, telepathic or supernatural powers) only and therefore won't perform 'magic tricks' in the traditional sense (tricks that require you to learn sleight of hand, say, or tricks with cleverly designed props). It goes both ways, too. People who perform the magic you've read about in the other eight chapters of this book won't usually claim to be psychic. I certainly don't.

Some of these distinctions can seem like they boil down to semantics or nit-picking, but I guess, from a performance point of view, you have to remember that a successful magician or mentalist has to create a believable, characterful persona on stage. If that persona is a 'person with extraordinary psychic and mental abilities' then it's based on the idea that you are special and different; hypnotic even. You have to convince the audience that you can do strange, paranormal, and otherworldly things just by using the power of your mind. Whereas with someone like me it's a bit more straightforward. You know rationally, for example, that I can't really squash one of my dancers until she's as thin as paper. I can't really teleport her in seconds to another part of the theatre. So I don't need to tell my audience, 'I can't really do this stuff.'

With mentalism, however, you need to make ethical choices when you start to perform the skills you've mastered. Do you claim to have genuine psychic powers and – by extension – the ability to connect with people living or dead? Or do you present these ideas for entertainment only? Derren Brown is a perfect example of someone who treads this fine line perfectly and ethically. He makes it entirely clear that he isn't really psychic. This was the disclaimer for his TV show; 'This programme fuses magic, suggestion, psychology, misdirection, and showmanship. I achieve all the results you'll see through a varied mixture of those techniques.'

The other ethical aspect is about money, because some people make a small fortune from claiming (and never deviating from the claim) that they have real psychic or spiritual abilities. But when you start learning about magic and mentalism, you learn that it's quite easy, with practice, to convince people that your powers are real.

And that's a lot of responsibility when you know that vulnerable, grieving, or ill people will – in desperation – seek out people who claim to have the answers. They'll pay good money for those answers, too. Obviously most people who perform mentalism acts find this sort of practice wildly immoral and irresponsible. To me, as

Above Unethical people have made a lot of money by convincing desperate people they have real psychic abilities.

a magician, I think it's okay to pretend you can talk to the dead, as long as you're not offering advice as part of that conversation or making it personal. For example, it's one thing to say, 'The ghost of Houdini is coming through and teaching me how to do this card trick.' But it's quite another to say, 'Your dead grandmother is coming through and telling me "It's okay, you have her blessing"'. That's a mean thing to do to people who are in mourning.

This tension – between people who use mentalism techniques as a form of entertainment and people who use them to take advantage of people – has always existed in magic. Charlatans, scammers, and liars have been challenged to prove their powers by magicians throughout history. Because they know how it's done, magicians have felt it was their duty to prove to people that it's really just a clever performance. The ethics have remained the same: 'Don't claim you have real powers'.

MIND READING AS ENTERTAINMENT

Mediumship has always been big business and, in many ways, it's easy to see why. Advances in science have uncovered many wonders of the human body but we still remain largely ignorant about the human brain. We don't know if our personalities are formed in our brain. We don't really know what makes us, as humans, conscious beings. The fact that the human brain is still an unknown quantity makes it fertile territory for a performer of mentalism. If we don't know what our brains are capable of, it's easy to sell the idea that you can do very strange and spooky things.

By the second half of the 19th century, mind reading had become a very popular form of entertainment. One way of making the act feel spookily real was to perform with someone you were related to. Husband and wife teams or brother and sister acts were able to suggest to their audience that blood relations or married couples had a special kind of mental bond (people often think this about twins, even today). One half of the pair would be blindfolded, while the other went out into the theatre, asking the audience to produce objects that belonged to them. The blindfolded performer would then be able to describe the objects, despite not seeing them. Thought-reading acts were also popular, with couples claiming to be able to transmit the name of a songs, places, dates, or even passages from a book to each other, just through the power of thought. Many couples used simple verbal codes to communicate the answers to each other in secret, but the codes were often hugely complicated and difficult to remember.

Above Born in Minnesota in 1880, C A Newmann started appearing in mind-reading and hypnotism shows at 13.

Opposite Mysterious gypsies with crystal balls crop up in countless stories and films.

PSYCHO KINETIC TOUCHES

If you're a performer, there's not really a distinction between what works close up and what works on stage – both kinds of mentalism involve a lot of the same principles and techniques. The only thing that's slightly harder is that in a small group you tend to need to be more accurate. In a close-up situation, the mind reader will have to use a method that lets him or her find out accurate information about one person, or the whole trick will have failed, whereas in front of a thousand people, I can say, 'I'm getting a message for someone called John,' and be relatively sure that there'll be at least one John in the audience. On stage, it's a more of a shotgun approach; you have a lot more leeway.

My favourite close-up mentalism act is called Psycho Kinetic Touches (or simply, PK Touches). David Blaine does a brilliant version of this for Will Smith and Jada Pinkett Smith that you can look up on YouTube. In this illusion, the mentalist will often pick two people from the audience who are related or in a relationship of some kind. Again, this is because the idea that couples are psychically linked – by love or by dint of knowing each other so well – is very powerful and somehow credible.

In the performance, you ask the two people to stand opposite each other, while you stand between them. They're usually a few feet apart – the idea is that they are nowhere near each other and certainly not touching, so they couldn't possibly know what is happening to the other person. The mentalist then asks one half of the couple (Person A) to close their eyes. If Person A feels a touch anywhere on the body, they must remember exactly where they felt it. Then the illusion begins.

The mentalist will go over to Person B and touch them in a specific place that is visible to the audience (say, the shoulder or an arm). The mentalist will then ask Person A if they could 'feel' the touch he made on Person B and, if so, where they felt it. Every time, Person A seems to know instinctively where on the body their partner was touched. They can physically feel the touch themselves.

Person A is then allowed to open their eyes and usually that's when the freaking out starts, 'But he didn't touch you!', 'I know!'.

It's a great illusion, particularly because it plays on our soppy, romantic inclinations. Just as people want to believe that there is 'The One' – that one person they will fall in love with forever – they also want to believe that people who love each other share a special, psychological connection. I'm not going to tell you what I think about either of those ideas; I don't want to spoil it for you.

Above People want to believe in 'The One' – that there is one person out there they will fall in love with forever.

MIND READING ON THE STAGE

If you search for vintage posters for magicians or mentalists you will definitely come across 'Alexander: The Man Who Knows'. The posters are stark, bold, and hugely collectable, which is fitting for a man who was one of the highest-paid entertainers of the 1920s. Accounts of his life are full of craziness, with some biographers claiming he was married as many as 14 times. Others say he once went on the run in a speedboat filled with counterfeit liquor or that he blackmailed an oil baron for $50,000. Let's just say he was quite a guy.

Claude 'Alexander' Conlin's act saw him dressed in exotic robes and a feathered turban, using a crystal ball to read the minds of members of the audience. It's worth contrasting this exotic, foreign presentation to someone like Derren Brown, who'll perform in a regular – if very well-cut – suit. Nowadays we say we can 'explain' the wonders of mind reading using ideas like subliminal messaging or NLP. But at the turn of the last century, Alexander's explanation was that he was special, mysterious, and from somewhere far, far away. Both modern and historic performers perform quite similar material though (both Alexander and Derren do what's called a Q&A act. These kinds of acts are very common in mentalism and are really effective).

The mind reader (usually blindfolded in some way) will 'read' the thoughts of people in the audience. Often they're asked to submit questions in sealed envelopes, which the mind reader will simply hold in his hand, unable to see them or open them. The mind reader might say, 'I'm thinking of a woman, born in the middle of May…' at which point, someone in the audience will say, 'Yes, that's me,' and then be told many personal things about themselves that the mentalist simply could not have known. The mind reader might also be able to guess a person's secret question and provide some kind of answer. It's the sheer number of people 'read' and given answers that makes an act like this impressive – it's often performed for an hour or longer, so you're constantly wondering

Opposite In order to appear more exotic, Claude 'Alexander' Conlin wore a feathered turban on stage.

BANACHEK

When he was 18 years old, self-taught mentalist Banachek (born 1960) managed to convince university scientists undertaking a paranormal research project that he possessed actual psychic powers – at least for a while, until they investigated his feats more closely and the hoax was made public. Banachek has since gone on to debunk others who claim to be psychics and faith healers.

He is the director of the JREF One Million Dollar Paranormal Challenge, set up by the stage magician and skeptic James Randi, which offers to pay out one million US dollars to anyone who can pass an agreed set of tests to prove they have paranormal or supernatural abilities. So far, not one of the hundreds of applicants has met the criteria.

how on earth the mentalist could know so much. Every revelation that hits home provokes gasps, so you have an amazing snowball of excitement in the room as the act progresses. 'Reading' a larger number of people also makes it unlikely that stooges have been used. If there were that many, the mind reader wouldn't make any money. And Alexander certainly did, earning millions of dollars during his career.

MY PREDICTION ILLUSIONS

Before, I explained a little about the differences between 'regular' magic tricks and mentalism, and why people usually specialize in one or the other. That's true of me, too. It's partly because mentalism is such a rich and in-depth field, so being an expert on it, as well as magic, would be really difficult. Also, when you read somebody's mind – especially if that person doesn't know anything about how it works – that can be a very freaky, almost invasive feeling for them. Your thoughts are the one thing you think are private and completely yours. When someone can apparently pluck one of those thoughts out, it can therefore be quite uncomfortable. And in a way that's a moral decision you have to face as a magician. I'm not the kind of person who's going to get super serious and dive into your thoughts – that's not the kind of performer I am. So I tend to focus on prediction effects where you foresee the outcome of something (lottery numbers, the numbers on a dollar bill). Or I'll do illusions where I prove I have a photographic memory, or that I'm a human calculator; that's about as far as I go. It's different to saying you're going to read someone's mind, because it's less heavy-handed and intimate.

In my TV special, the Prediction illusion I did went like this: I start by placing my wallet on a tall table at one side of the stage. I'm going to leave it in full view of the audience for the whole act, so I tell the audience to keep an eye on it. Then I give the audience a clue to where we're going. I talk about coincidence and how rare and special it is when two incidents fall in line perfectly with

With prediction illusions, I prefer to focus on lottery numbers rather than invading people's private thoughts.

one another. The music starts and I pick up my Nerf machine gun, which has fat foam bullets I can shoot harmlessly into the audience. Picking an audience member at random is different for every magician (Derren Brown sometimes uses a Frisbee, David Copperfield has used beach balls), but this is how I like to do it. For this trick, I'm sending eight missiles into the audience so everyone knows that I can't decide who gets them, it's all down to chance. I point the Nerf gun high into the air and fire it, the first missile lands and I ask the person to name a two-digit number – any number up to 99. The crowd loves it, it's like trying to catch the baseball at a major league game – everyone wants to get picked.

I ask everyone who caught a missile to stand up. Then, one by one, I ask each audience member to name their number, which I write one after the other on a huge white card. It's nice to get the opportunity to interact with your audience, so this part is cool, because it feels like we're doing something together, it's a nice relaxed atmosphere. Obviously it also makes it clear to everybody again that no one standing up is employed by me – their reactions and what they say are unscripted and natural. By the end of it, we've got a 16-digit number, selected totally randomly. I display the number on big screens so you can see it even if you're sitting way up in the back. 'The chances of this working are literally a trillion to one,' I say.

Then I'm walking over to the other side of the stage where my wallet's still on the table. I tend to ask an assistant to help me get it because there's something less suspect about another person handling the wallet rather than me, and the audience already has a clue where I'm going with all this. So I get them to get out my credit card and check it's real – feel it, bend it a little, check it's legit. Then I ask them to read out the long number on the card, one by one, nice and slow. If I can, I make sure there's a camera on the card too, so everyone can see that the number really is on the card and we're not just cheating. Unbelievably, the number on the card is the same as the 16-digit number selected by the audience. Everyone goes crazy.

WHY DOES MIND READING WORK?

'For those who believe, no explanation is necessary. For those who don't, none will suffice'

That's Joseph Dunninger, who performed as a mentalist on radio and television from the 1940s to the 1960s. It's how he would sign off his show, though strangely the quote itself is attributed to a 13th-century monk, Thomas Aquinas ('To one who has faith, no explanation is necessary. To one without faith, no explanation is possible.') Whoever came up with it, what I love about the phrase is that it explains what you're faced with when you perform mind-reading illusions. Because some people believe it's possible to 'read' people (and maybe they believe in the paranormal, too), there's no amount of proof you could give them that would change their mind. Even if you exposed them to how mentalism works, or gave them 20 books on the subject, they would find another 'psychic' to believe in – they simply won't believe it's a trick. Then, of course, on the other hand, you've got the sceptics. The people who don't buy into anything religious, spiritual, or supernatural – well, no illusion could make those people believe. So how do you make sure they still have a great time when they come to see your show?

Above Joseph Dunninger performed on radio and TV from the 1940s to the 1960s.

MAGICAL EXPLANATIONS

If you had to write a timeline for what happens in someone's head after they've been fooled by a magic trick, it might go something like this:

1. Sees inexplicable thing
2. Experiences moment of wonder
3. Wants to know how it's done
4. Starts to think up theories
5. Theories don't quite work

What happens next? You either a) accept the illusion, or b) get annoyed. Acceptance is hard to achieve though, because you can't square the circle in your mind. Being annoyed is even worse, because if you can't figure out the method it can make you feel stupid. Sometimes, this anger is directed at the magician, because people assume the magician is arrogant/thinks they're better than everyone. Either way, neither of these outcomes is particularly good news – for the magician or the audience. That's why magicians use false explanations.

FAUXSPLAINING

Magicians and mentalists have always tried to work out the optimum amount of science to include when explaining their tricks. For example, if we look at the history of levitation, you'll see early performers using science to explain how people could float. If you've read the Levitation chapter (see pages 54–75) you'll know that for the magician Robert-Houdin, it was the chemical ether – then an unknown gas that had strange properties attributed to it. Robert-Houdin's son inhaled ether and then rose in a ghostly sleep to a horizontal position, suspended in air. So for Houdin's audience, it was the ether that did it.

Now look again at Derren Brown's elegant explanation for his TV show. He uses disclaimers like this quite often and they're often deliberately worded in a brilliant way. What does he claim is the method for his magic? It's 'magic, suggestion, psychology, misdirection and showmanship.' Now think about it. How many of these concepts are you intimately familiar with? And what does 'showmanship' really mean?

PSEUDO SCIENCE

Pseudo science is the blanket term we tend use when we want to describe some thing as half-science and half-nonsense. It's those wild stories in the news that are based on tiny scientific studies, the ones that don't really have a basis in fact. Pseudo science is not science we can respect; it's not been peer-reviewed or published in a respected journal. It's that suspicious feeling you get when someone is telling you about a new beauty breakthrough, miracle cream, or fad diet. You're putting what on your skin? You're eating what?

You've only got to look at cosmetic companies and the pseudo-scientific language they use to sell face creams. A more recent trend would be all the books and websites devoted to hacking your brain and body – making yourself smarter through diet (like 'bulletproof' or paleo coffee) or by taking certain kinds of (usually

'Magicians use false explanations ... early performers used science to explain how people could float'

very expensive) vitamins. I'm not saying that all of these things don't work, but some of it is definitely meaningless nonsense.

Complicated jargon and the air of science can give ideas legitimacy and make it seem like they could work. This is also very true of magic and, more specifically, mentalism. If you can give the audience a pseudo-scientific explanation for how you read the minds of your audience, or got them to say/write/draw specific things, that makes it much more satisfying to the audience. It takes it away from it being a cheap trick, and at the same time you're stroking the intellect of the audience, 'Oh yeah, you're smart people, of course you know about NLP/body language/subliminal messaging.'

All I'm doing, then, is showing the audience what you can do with those theories. When you speak to people this way it also means you're more likely to have the audience onside; it's a form of intellectual camaraderie, a kind of 'we're all smart people here'. Nobody is likely to say, 'No, I don't know anything about that form of psychology or science,' because they don't want to embarrass themselves. It's like on *Jimmy Kimmel Live!* when they go out on the street at music festivals like Coachella and do vox pops with members of the public. They'll make up the names of bands and ask people if they're into that band or if they dug their show. Everyone just says, 'OMG, they were amazing,' rather than admit they haven't heard of these made-up bands. Nobody wants to look uncool or stupid.

Above Complicated jargon and the air of science can give wild ideas legitimacy.

PSEUDO SCIENCE & EGO

Often with pseudo science you're also dealing with theories that people really, really want to believe are true. Say you're a smoker and you want to give up smoking – the chances are that you've already tried to quit a million times. You know how hard it is. So if someone tells you that all you have to do is go to a couple of hypnotherapy sessions, you're going to want to believe it. I'm not saying hypnotherapy doesn't work for people, but a large part of it working may be down to the fact that they really, really want it to. It's like the placebo effect.

This is true of any theory that claims to make us smarter, thinner, more beautiful, or healthier. The sheer amount of desire at play, how much we want to be better, makes us susceptible to flimsy science. So many people buy into these ideas and don't fully investigate them because they've got just the right amount – the perfect percentage – of credibility to them. When an idea or theory seems just on the outskirts of possibility, why not try it? Because, what if it's true? If we're honest with ourselves, so many of these pseudo-scientific theories rely on elements of our ego – having low self-esteem, being greedy or selfish, or maybe just simply a good, honest desire to be better. All these ideas, ingredients, and theories also rely on the fact we need change to be easy.

BODY LANGUAGE & POKER TELLS

A really great example of an idea that people commonly use for an explanation in magic (and not just in mentalism) is body language. People often bring it up when you're doing any kind of card trick where you have to guess or 'mind read' what card they picked. You'll study their face hard and say, 'I think it's a red suit. Yes, it's definitely hearts or diamonds.' They become convinced – without you needing to say anything – that somehow they communicated what suit their card was, by their face. Which is fantastic in a way, because as long as your audience is thinking that your secret is something to do with how they flared their nostrils or moved their eyes, you can guarantee they're not going to work out how you really did it.

Also, the great thing about an idea like body language, or poker 'tells' is that it's an idea I could probably guarantee that 90 per cent of my audience has heard of. Crucially, the number of them that actually own and have read a book on the subject is far, far smaller. It's an idea that's entered the public consciousness. So we will know snippets. We know that we give out non-verbal cues so people can tell if we're shy or confident. We know poker 'tells' are small micro-expressions or movements that people display if they're lying. We know if you look to the right when you're talking you're lying, because it shows you're using the right side of your brain, where we imagine and create thoughts. These ideas are so interesting, novel, and neat to us; why would we spoil it by reading the original scientific research papers? Do they even exist? And can you communicate the colour red with your nose?

'These ideas are so interesting, novel, and neat to us; why would we spoil it by reading the original scientific research papers?'

SWITCHING IT UP

The last thing that's important when using a phony explanation for your illusion is that magicians and mind readers can't rest on their laurels for long. We have to change what scientific theories we use, as the public gets smarter and more aware. This means that although whatever's in pop culture or popular science at any one time should be considered for your phony explanation, you need to keep up. Popular science theories change all the time, so what we used ten years ago won't necessarily work today.

Opposite Poker 'tells' are a great example of reading body language to your advantage.

MENTALISM & PERSONAL ATTENTION

Let's go back to the Q&A act. In it, members of the audience are asked to write down a question they would like to be answered by the mind reader. See if you can think of a question like that now. Make it a question related to your life that you'd really like help with. Maybe it's something to do with the relationship you're in or the fact that you're not in one and would like to be. Maybe it's about your job and whether you'll get that promotion. Some mentalists insist on you making them very personal questions because that makes the feelings and thoughts more 'powerful'; they'll be able to read them better that way.

Below The more details psychics are able to give you, the more likely you are to believe them – especially if what they are telling you is favourable.

How does this inform the success of the act? Well first, you have to remember that anyone picked and asked to talk about themselves in front of a room full of strangers will likely feel a little bit special and a little bit vulnerable. If they have to stand up, it'll make them more nervous (public speaking is one of the most common phobias), making them easier to manipulate. It's also true to say that this is a very rare situation – there aren't many moments in adult life where you are the centre of attention. We live in a world where our individual uniqueness is slowly getting stripped away – the internet shows us that whatever social class or fashion 'tribe' we belong to, there are thousands of people just like us.

This rare sense of personal attention hones right in on our ego. You feel a similar thing if you go and have a facial, or have your palm read, or go to see a psychic – you become the focus of the room. And this weird 'spotlighting' has the power to change you from a cynic to a believer. Someone has picked you out of an entire theatre audience; the balance of power has changed. You begin to view the information the mind reader gives you differently just because it's about you. You also give more weight to the details he claims to be able to 'read' about you; especially if they're favourable ('You're a very creative person'/'You do too much for other people.'). The mind reader might have been 'lucky' when he got some facts right about everyone else, but *it's different when he's right about you.*

It's also worth remembering that the question you're thinking about or have written down probably has huge emotional resonance for you (love, work, family). You're just human; everyone's looking for answers (usually to the same questions). So there's something really attractive about somebody who claims to know everything. Lots of people shy away from making big changes – whether to get divorced, have another child, or move house in order to take job – because they seem so final and terrifying. So it's a relief to have somebody make those decisions for you. It reminds me a little of how people pour their heart out to a hairdresser. But acting on the advice given by a stranger (mind reader or not) could be very, very foolish.

PEER PRESSURE AND CONFORMITY

As adults, we like to believe we are free thinkers, unswayed by the adverts we see on television, firm in our beliefs. The interesting thing that performing magic teaches you, though, is that people rarely question authority. If I am confident and calm, I could even present you with something you knew was wrong, but you'd still agree with me in public. It's not that you're weak, either. It's because you're human.

The Asch experiments demonstrate this public weakness perfectly. Carried out by psychologist Solomon Asch in 1951, these were studies in group behaviour that tested whether people could be swayed by the 'herd'. In groups, participants were presented with two white cards. On Card A there was a thick black line. On Card B there were three lines, one of which clearly matched the length of the line on Card A. All subjects had to do was choose which of the three lines on Card B matched the line on Card A. Crucially, though, they had to give their answer publicly, after the rest of a group had given theirs.

Above People are easily swayed by 'herd' behaviour and will follow authority figures unquestioningly.

Opposite In as series of experiments, Soloman Asch showed that many people would rather go along with the majority than risk looking stupid in front of others.

The rest of each group, however, were stooges who confidently gave the wrong answer. What Asch found was that over 12 trials, 75 per cent of people conformed at least once with the majority and gave the wrong answer. When they were questioned after, subjects were happy to say that they knew it was the wrong answer when they gave it. They were just worried about looking stupid, so agreed with the group.

If you apply this to a mind-reading performance, it could certainly help things along. It doesn't mean when the mind reader says; 'Your star sign is Aquarius and you like fishing as a hobby' that everyone will agree, but it'll certainly work if the 'readings' are less specific, and it'll certainly work a percentage of the time. You'll also notice some mind readers say, 'Yes?' after each pronouncement. Again, put yourself in the shoes of the person who's standing in front of everyone, and think about how little time they have to act and disagree if the observation/ prediction made by the mind reader is wrong. It takes a strong personality to say, 'No, you're wrong.'

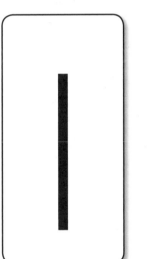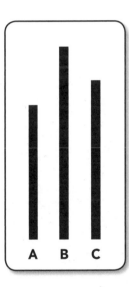

Of course, this leaves the audience to make a natural assumption: that everything the mind reader says is correct. After all, the audience likely only hears when the predictions are correct (because in contrast, when he gets it right the chosen person will say 'Yes, that's right,' because they're excited). This win–win situation means that unless you know everyone in the audience, or are willing to spend the entire interval asking everyone in the theatre whether the mentalist was really right about them, you'll never really know.

You'll never really know. Magic in a nutshell.

illusion

IT'S ALL AN ILLUSION... OR IS IT?

MON	TUES	WED	THUR	FRI	SAT	SUN
1	2	3	4	5	6	7
8	9	10	11	12	13	14
15	16	17	18	19	20	21
22	23	24	25	26	27	28
29	30					

I'd like you to draw a box that goes 4 numbers across and 4 numbers down, anywhere in the calendar. Inside your box you'll end up with 16 numbers, but it's your choice where you place the box.

Circle any number you'd like within that box, then cross out all the numbers in the same row and column as the one you circled. Next, circle another number that hasn't already been crossed out, before crossing out all the numbers in the same row and column. Do this one more time; circle any remaining number, and cross out all the other numbers in the same row and column. You should be left with one number that isn't crossed out, so go ahead and circle that too.

Add up the four numbers you've circled. Keep in mind, YOU chose where to draw the box. YOU chose the numbers to circle. This number you've arrived at – the total of your four circled numbers – has been completely random, but under YOUR control... Now turn to that page in the book, and look at the first word of the first paragraph on that page...

Now, look inside my ear on page 214... Notice anything? This word is planted in images throughout the book. How many can you find, including this one? Go to www.darcyoake.com to find out more!

INDEX

PICTURE CREDITS

Picture Researcher: Sophie Hartley

Special photography: © Mark Harrison p 10, 28, 34, 53, 54, 61, 76, 98, 103, 120, 123, 137, 142, 157, 164, 183, 192, 214

Other Photography:
Alamy AF Archive 71; blickwinkel/Henning 212; Chris Cheadle 187; Everett Collection Historical 171, 181; Grenville Collins Postcard Collection/Chronicle 58; H. Armstrong Roberts/ClassicStock 97; Hero Images Inc. 116; James Grady 72; K-PHOTOS 161; Martin Bond 23; Moviestore Collection Ltd. 37; Oote Boe 1 122; Pictorial Press Ltd. 27, 172; Prospero 184; Quim Roser/Age Fotostock 117; Sarah Edwards/WENN Ltd. 20, 177; Sonja Krebs/imageBROKER 140; SOTK2011 109; WENN Ltd. 45; ZUMA Press, Inc. 92, 101. Bridgeman Images © Museum of the City of New York, USA 15; Private Collection/Photo © Christie's Images 110. Christie Goodwin 7, 119. Corbis 87, 203. Courtesy of Darcy Oake 186. FremantleMedia Limited/Simco Limited 178. Getty Images APIC 57, 67, 111, 170; Archive Photos 102; Barry Brecheisen 83; Bob Thomas 48; Buyenlarge 64; Central Press 167; Chris Ware/Keystone Features 66; Cristian Baitg 75; DeAgostini 14, 18; Ethan Miller 130; Fei Yang 158; General Photographic Agency 193; Hulton Archive 68, 107, 194, 206; Ken Faught/Toronto Star via Getty Images 30; Kevin Winter/ACM2009/Getty Images for ACM 38; Larry Busacca/Getty Images for the 2014 Tribeca Film Festival 16; Michael Stuparyk/Toronto Star via Getty Images 148; NBC/NBCU Photo Bank via Getty Images 82; Pascal Le Segretain 24; Paul Drinkwater/NBC/NBCU Photo Bank 124; Popperfoto 129, 168; Rosie Hallam/Barcroft Media 69; Sam Greenfield/Dongfeng Race Team/Volvo Ocean Race via Getty Images 162; Thurston Hopkins/Picture Post 134; travelstock44/LOOK-foto 210; ullstein bild/ullstein bild via Getty Images 33, 39. Harry Ransom Center, The University of Texas at Austin 152. iStock 4x6 47, 141; Marilyn Nieves 94; mediaphotos 208. ITV 40, 63, 84. Library of Congress 51, 59, 105, 195, 199. Manuel Sousa Photography 154. Mary Evans Picture Library Peter & Dawn Cope Collection 79. Rex Features 112, 126; ITV 89 above, 89 below; Keith Waldegrave/Associated Newspapers 147; Ken McKay 81; Sipa Press 80, 151. Shutterstock 3445128471 114; Adrian Reynolds 145; Alila Medical Media 49; AVAVA 90; Everett Collection 12, 149; KarSol 43; Lightboxx 200; mikeledray 139; Petrenko Andriy 197; Phase4Studios 4 (used throughout); urbanbuzz 201. TopFoto Marilyn Kingwill/ArenaPAL 204.

CREDITS

Commissioning Editor   Hannah Knowles

Writing and Research   Wendy Roby

Layout Design   Clarkevanmeurs Design Limited

Designer   Jaz Bahra

Senior Editor   Alex Stetter

Picture Researcher   Sophie Hartley

Illustrations   Grace Helmer

Special Photography   Mark Harrison

Senior Production Manager   Peter Hunt